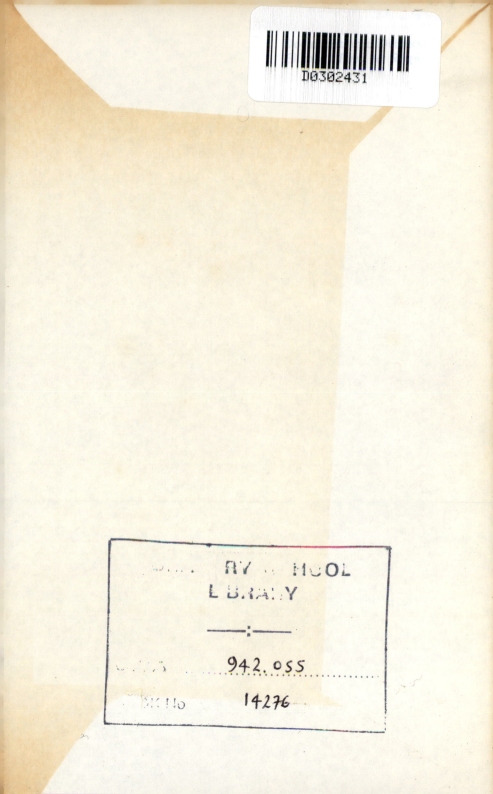

Documents and Debates
General Editor: John Wroughton M.A., F.R.Hist.S.

Elizabeth I and her Reign

Richard Salter

MACMILLAN
EDUCATION

First published 1988

Published by
MACMILLAN EDUCATION LTD
Houndmills, Basingstoke, Hampshire RG21 2XS
and London
Companies and representatives
throughout the world

Typeset by Wessex Typesetters
(Division of The Eastern Press Ltd)
Frome, Somerset

Printed in Hong Kong

British Library Cataloguing in Publication Data
Salter, Richard
Elizabeth I and her reign.—(Documents
and debates).
1. Great Britain—History—
Elizabeth, 1558–1603
I. Title II. Series
942.05′5   DA257
ISBN 0–333–42381–X

Contents

General Editor's Preface

This book forms part of a series entitled *Documents and Debates*, which is aimed primarily at sixth formers. The earlier volumes in the series each covered approximately one century of history, using material both from original documents and from modern historians. The more recent volumes, however, are designed in response to the changing trends in history examinations at 18 plus, most of which now demand the study of documentary sources and the testing of historical skills. Each volume therefore concentrates on a particular topic within a narrower span of time. It consists of eight sections, each dealing with a major theme in depth, illustrated by extracts drawn from primary sources. The series intends partly to provide experience for those pupils who are required to answer questions on documentary material at A-level, and partly to provide pupils of all abilities with a digestible and interesting collection of source material, which will extend the normal textbook approach.

This book is designed essentially for the pupil's own personal use. The author's introduction will put the period as a whole into perspective, highlighting the central issues, main controversies, available source material and recent developments. Although it is clearly not our intention to replace the traditional textbook, each section will carry its own brief introduction, which will set the documents into context. A wide variety of source material has been used in order to give the pupils the maximum amount of experience – letters, speeches, newspapers, memoirs, diaries, official papers, Acts of Parliament, Minute Books, accounts, local documents, family papers, etc. The questions vary in difficulty, but aim throughout to compel the pupil to think in depth by the use of unfamiliar material. Historical knowledge and understanding will be tested, as well as basic comprehension. Pupils will also be encouraged by the questions to assess the reliability of evidence, to recognise bias and emotional prejudice, to reconcile conflicting accounts and to extract the essential from the irrelevant. Some questions, *marked with an asterisk*, require knowledge outside the immediate extract and are intended for further research or discussion, based on the pupil's general knowledge of the period. Finally, we hope that students using this material will learn something of the nature of historical inquiry and the role of the historian.

John Wroughton

Acknowledgements

The author and publishers wish to thank the following who have kindly given permission for the use of copyright material:

The British Library for extracts from archive material; Catholic Record Society for an extract from *The Wisbech Stirs, 1595–8*, ed. P. Renold, vol LI, 1958; The Folger Institute for extracts from *The Description of England William Harrison 1577* ed. Georges Edelen, Cornell University Press, 1968; Hakluyt Society for an extract from *New Light on Drake*, ed. Zelia Nuttall, Second Series, vol 34, 1914; Longman Group (UK) Ltd for an extract from *English Historical Review*, ed. J. E. Neale, vol 65, 1950; Thomas Nelson and Sons Ltd for an extract from *A Source Book of Scottish History 1567–1707*, eds Dickinson and Donaldson, vol III, 1954; Oxford University Press for extracts from *The Memoirs of Richard Carey*, ed. F. H. Mares, copyright OUP, 1972; H. C. Porter for an extract from *Puritanism in Tudor England*, Macmillan, 1970; Deborah Rogers Ltd on behalf of the author for an extract from *The Other Face: Catholic Life Under Elizabeth I*, ed. P. Caraman, Longman, 1960; Royal Historical Society for 'The Count of Feria's dispatch to Philip II, 14 November 1558', eds M. J. Rodriguez-Salgado and S. Adams, *Camden Miscellany XXVIII*, Camden Fourth Series, vol 29, 1984; Somerset Record Office for extracts from archive material.

Every effort has been made to trace all the copyright holders but if any have been inadvertently overlooked the publishers will be pleased to make the necessary arrangement at the first opportunity.

Elizabeth I and her Reign

Do we still believe that 'ages' in history begin and end with the deaths and accessions of monarchs? Was there in fact an 'Elizabethan Age'?

Elizabeth's subjects would certainly have experienced a unity in their lives which the chapters of a book belie. I hope that some sense of that unity leaps the divisions which this book necessarily contains. There are strong links between Chapters 3, 4 and 5, concerning the economy, poverty and protest. Preoccupations with affairs in Ireland, Scotland and Europe (Chapters 7 and 8) entered the field of politics, taxation and even, in the extreme crises, day-to-day life in the coastal and border regions. Catholics and Protestants, famous and lowly, expressed themselves in frankly religious terms in every sphere of life. Religious motivations permeated especially the activities of parliament.

Yet is the reign itself a 'unity' set apart from the time before and the time after? I have thrown a little extra emphasis on two periods of Elizabeth's reign in a number of documents scattered through the book. Some relate to the start of the reign. Philip II and Spain were friendly: France was a dangerous enemy: turmoil in Scotland had an uncertain outcome: rebellions were yet to turn Ireland into a kind of enemy and Holland into a kind of friend: Elizabeth's attitudes to religion and parliament were unclear: her chosen advisers, set against the Marian bishops and councillors, were inexperienced: Elizabeth was expected to marry – is not the period from the 1540s to the 1560s essentially one? Another scattering of documents relates to the 1590s. There was economic crisis: there were severe challenges to the balance of politics: conflict between Elizabeth, her courtiers and her parliaments: the war with Spain went badly. Do not these themes foreshadow the reigns of James and Charles?

So, if there was a unity of action in Elizabeth's reign, and if the first and last years of the reign suggest a unity with the times before and after, does not the reign itself have an identity, and have historians always seen this identity in the same light?

In the beginnings of Elizabethan history, chronicle, myth and legend intertwine. Images of Elizabeth as 'Gloriana', or the 'Faerie Queene', and hardly less romantic images of Leicester, Hawkins,

Drake, Essex and Raleigh, established the queen as a 'larger than life' character. Even more remarkable legends have arisen over the centuries. At Eglwyseg, near Llangollen, Elizabeth is supposed to have been confined in pregnancy in 1563, while at Bisley in the Cotswolds she is supposed to have been a changeling boy (these two legends have at any rate the obliging effect of cancelling each other out!) More sober historians born in her own reign soon began to write the history of her reign in the light of Stuart history. Camden and Naunton particularly throw aspects of Elizabeth's policy into relief in such a way as to imply criticism of the statescraft of James I or Charles I. Much later, from the viewpoint of late Victorian self-confidence, historians such as Pollard and Creighton see in Elizabeth's reign the birth of a nation. Some twentieth-century historians, such as Rowse and Neale, have continued to draw Elizabethan history along the same eulogistic road, not from the vantage point of national self-confidence but from the sense of the comparison that could be drawn between sixteenth and twentieth-century England as a nation under threat from potent enemies and alien ideologies.

Seeing the past still, no doubt, as our forebears did, through the eyes of the present, but now from the wry and sceptical viewpoint of the late twentieth century, we have made some revisions to Elizabethan history. If Mary Tudor and James I were less inept than they were once supposed to be, does not Elizabeth's star shine a little less brightly by comparison? Detailed researches have suggested that the religious reformation in England was slower, later and less complete than formerly thought: that violence and poverty were as endemic in Elizabeth's England as before and after: that the 'consensus' in politics was very brittle. We are less ready now to seek the causes of the Civil War in Elizabeth's reign, as past debates including that of 'the gentry' have done.

The mention of research raises the question of evidence. Modern historians, particularly in the economic sphere, 'make' much of their evidence by statistical analysis of numerous details. This evidence is extremely valuable but liable to modern bias and selectivity, and to errors in interpretation. Analysis of money values is particularly vulnerable in this way. From among contemporary written sources it is difficult to make a balanced selection because the chances of survival are far greater for documents supportive of the Elizabethan regime: documents that find their way into state papers and noble family archives are generally 'conformist' in this way or, if they are not, such as 'libels' and intercepted letters, they appear as if isolated and rendered harmless by a hostile context, like flies in amber. The best sources of genuinely critical comment on Elizabeth's England, neutral or hostile, are foreign sources.

So what events and movements were essentially Elizabethan?

Readers may criticise or add to this tentative list: the establishment of the Church of England: a diplomatic revolution which made Spain the enemy instead of France: political and religious changes which converted Scotland from an alien enemy to a not-yet-quite comfortable neighbour: the emergence of a new nation (Holland), at once a potential friend and rival: systematic treatment of economic affairs and poor relief by statute: a literary flowering: and of course the personality and impact of a remarkable woman.

I 'All the Men and Women Merely Players' – Personalities

Introduction

The forces which shaped and changed Tudor England were powerful, but they were not impersonal. The great changes which occurred in religion, in the balance of power in Europe, in the economy, in art, fashion and manners affected and were affected by the lives of countless men and women, famous and forgotten.

We must beware, however, of a tendency to overpersonalise, and thereby at times to trivialise, some of the events of the times. English views of Spanish, Scottish and Irish history are marred by this tendency (see extract *a* of Section 9 in this chapter). Glorification of the exploits of Hawkins and Drake has at times led to an overestimate of England's power and importance in the world, besides blinding us to errors of judgement made at times by Elizabeth, her councillors and commanders.

Debates about the significance of personality are particularly significant in the question of 'faction'. The historiography of faction in Elizabethan England began within very few years of the queen's death, as William Camden and Sir Robert Naunton presented her as the mistress and manipulator of faction, an interpretation of the reign developed and refined in modern times by J. E. Neale, W. T. MacCaffrey and J. Hurstfield. That there were clashes of motive, interest, personality and political and religious stance among Elizabeth's courtiers and councillors is undeniable, yet the proposition that the queen sustained and benefited from faction is barren. Elizabeth, strong-willed as she was, can have gained nothing by divisions among her ministers that she could not have gained by their unanimity.

History has always its chance cards. Just as Sir Robert Walpole remained so long in power partly because he outlived his early rivals, so we owe the very existence of a 'reign of Elizabeth' to the accident that, contrary to expectations, she survived her half-sister by 35 years.

1 From the Tower to the Throne

(a) [Original in German.]

In this very palace [Woodstock] the present reigning Queen
Elizabeth, before she was confined to the Tower, was kept
prisoner by her sister Mary; while she was detained here in the
utmost peril of her life, she wrote with a piece of charcoal the
5 following verses, composed by herself, upon a window shutter:

> O Fortune! how thy restless wavering state
>   Hath fraught with cares my troubled wit!
> Witness this present prison whither fate
>   Hath borne me, and the joys I quit.
> 10 Thou causedest the guilty to be loosed
> From bonds, wherewith are innocents enclosed;
>   Causing the guiltless to be strait reserved,
> And freeing those that death had well deserved:
> But by her envy can be nothing wrought,
> 15 So God send to my foes all they have thought.
>   ELIZABETH PRISONER
>   A.D. MDLV

[Elizabeth was held at Woodstock *after* the Tower]
     Paul Hentzner, *Travels in England During the Reign of Queen
     Elizabeth*, trans. Horace Walpole (London, 1797), p. 45

(b) [Original in Spanish.]

I arrived here on Wednesday the ninth of this month at lunchtime
20 and found the Queen our Lady's health to be just as Dr. Nunez
describes in his letter to your Majesty. There is, therefore, no
hope of her life, but on the contrary, each hour I think that they
will come to inform me of her death, so rapidly does her condition
deteriorate from one day to the next. She was happy to see me,
25 since I brought her news of your Majesty, and to receive the
letter, although she was unable to read it. In view of this, I felt
there was no time to waste on other matters and sent word to the
Council to assemble as I wished to talk to them on your Majesty's
behalf. . . . [He discusses Elizabeth's succession and the negotiations
30 over Calais.] . . . These councillors are extremely frightened of
what Madam Elizabeth will do with them. They have received me
well, but somewhat as they would a man who came with bulls
from a dead pope.
    The day after I arrived, I went to a house belonging to a
35 gentleman some 23 miles from here, where Madam Elizabeth is
staying. [Probably Sir John Brockett's Brockett Hall, Hertfordshire.] I arrived there some time before she might wish to
dine and she received me well, although not as joyfully as she did

the last time. She asked me to dine with her, and the wife of
40   Admiral Clinton who was there when I arrived was also invited.
During the meal we laughed and enjoyed ourselves a great deal.
After dinner she rose and told me that should I desire to speak
with her I might do so now, for she was giving orders that only
two or three women who could speak no other language than
45   English should remain in the room. I replied that I would prefer
the whole kingdom to hear what I wished to say to her, for it was
only to repeat what I had told her the last time of the goodwill
and brotherly love that she would always find in your Majesty,
and to prove to her the truth of what I had declared before and
50   was now repeating, I offered to show her an instruction that your
Majesty had given to me, written in your own hand . . . .
    I introduced a number of topics in my discourse to see how she
would respond to them. She was very open with me on many
points, much more that I would have expected, and although it is
55   difficult to judge a person one has known for as short a time as I
have known this woman, I shall tell your Majesty what I have
been able to gather. She is a very vain and clever woman. She
must have been thoroughly schooled in the manner in which her
father conducted his affairs, and I am very much afraid that she
60   will not be well-disposed in matters of religion, for I see her
inclined to govern through men who are believed to be heretics
and I am told that all the women around her definitely are. Apart
from this, it is evident that she is highly indignant about what has
been done to her during the Queen's lifetime. She puts great store
65   by the people and is very confident that they are all on her side,
which is certainly true. She declares that it was the people who
put her in her present position [i.e. at liberty] and she will not
acknowledge that your Majesty or the nobility of the realm had any
part in it, although, as she herself says, they have all sent her
70   assurances of their loyalty. In fact there is not a heretic or a traitor
in all the kingdom who has not joyfully raised himself from the
grave in order to come to her side. She is determined to be
governed by no one . . . .

    'The Count of Feria's dispatch to Philip II, 14 Nov 1558' eds
    M. J. Rodriguez-Salgado and S. Adams, *Camden Miscellany
    XXVIII* (Camden Society, 1985), pp 328–30

Questions

★   *a*   What reasons had Queen Mary for imprisoning her sister
Elizabeth?
★   *b*   By reference to other primary and secondary sources, comment
on the reliability of Hentzner's account of Elizabeth's imprisonment.

c Compare Feria's outlook (extract *b*) with that of Sir Nicholas Throckmorton (Chapter 6, Section 1*a*).

d In what matters could Feria's actions have been construed as foreign interference?

e Were the Marian councillors' fears justified by events? (Compare extract *b*, lines 30–1, with Chapter 6, Section 1*b*).

f What evidence is there in extract *b* of Elizabeth's command of languages?

★ *g* Why might Philip feel injured by Elizabeth's declaration that 'it was the people who put her in her present position' (extract *b*, lines 66–7)? (See also Section 4.)

★ *h* How prophetic was the last sentence of extract *b*?

2 From Youth to Age

(a) [Elizabeth] was of person tall, of hair and complexion fair, and therewith well favoured, but high-nosed; of limbs and features neat; and, which added to the lustre of these external graces, of a stately and majestic comportment, participating in this more of
5 her father than of her mother. . . . If we search further into her intellectuals and abilities, the wheel-course of her government deciphers them to the admiration of posterity; for it was full of magnanimity, tempered with justice, piety and pity, and to speak truth, noted but with one act of stain or taint, all her deprivations,
10 either of life or liberty, being legal and necessitated. She was learned, her sex and time considered, beyond common belief; for letters about this time, or somewhat before, did but begin to be of esteem and in fashion, the former ages being overcast with the mists and fogs of the Roman ignorance . . . . Her ministers and
15 instruments of state were many and those memorable, but they were only favourites, and not minions; such as acted more by her princely rules and judgments than by their own wills and appetites . . . . The principal note of her reign will be, that she ruled much by faction and parties, which she herself made, upheld
20 and weakened, as her own great judgment advised . . . .

> Sir Robert Naunton, *Fragmenta Regalia, (1641)* (London, 1797), pp 79–82

(b) She was a Lady upon whom nature had bestowed, and well placed, many of her fairest favours; of stature mean, slender, straight and amiably composed: of such state in her carriage as every motion of her seemed to bear majesty; her hair was inclined
25 to pale yellow, her forehead large and fair, a seeming set for princely grace; her eyes lively and sweet, but short-sighted; her nose somewhat rising in the middle; the whole compass of her countenance somewhat long, but yet of admirable beauty, not so

much in that which is termed the flower of youth, as in a most
30   delightful composition of majesty and modesty in equal mixture.
But without good qualities of mind, the gifts of nature are like
painted flowers, without either virtue or sap: yea, sometimes they
grow horrid and loathsome. Now her virtues were such as might
suffice to make an Æthiopian beautiful, which the more a man
35   knows and understands, the more he shall admire and love. In life,
she was most innocent; in desires, moderate; in purpose, just; of
spirit, above credit and almost capacity of her sex; of divine wit,
as well for depth of judgment as for quick conceit and speedy
expedition; of eloquence, as sweet in the utterance, so ready and
40   easy to come to the utterance; of wonderful knowledge both in
learning and affrays; skilful not only in the Latin and Greek, but
also in diverse other foreign languages; none knew better the
hardest art of all others, that is, of commanding men, nor could
more use themselves to those cares without which the royal
45   dignity could not be supported. She was religious, magnanimous,
merciful and just; respective of the honour of others, and exceeding
tender in the touch of her own. She was lovely and loving, the
two principal bands of duty and obedience . . . . She was rather
liberal than magnificent, making good choice of the receivers; and
50   for this cause was thought weak by some against the desire for
money. But it is certain that, beside the want of treasure which
she found, her continual affairs in Scotland, France, the Low
Countries and in Ireland, did occasion great provision of money,
which could not be better supplied than by cutting off either
55   excessive or unnecessary expense at home. Excellent Queen! What
do my words but wrong thy worth? What do I do but gild
gold? . . .

> Sir John Hayward, *Annals of the first four years of the reign of
> Queen Elizabeth*, ed. J. Bruce (Camden Society, 1840),
> pp 6–8

(c) [Original in German.]

. . . In the afternoon of the 18th August [1592] he [The Duke of
Württemburg] had another audience of her Majesty on which
60   occasion she herself made and delivered an appropriate speech, in
the presence of M. de Beauvois [the French Ambassador], in the
French language, which, together with many others, her Majesty
understands and speaks very well; and since, as before said, her
Majesty held M. de Beauvois in especial favour, after he had been
65   conversing with her Majesty very lively and good humouredly,
he so far prevailed upon her that she played very sweetly and
skilfully on her instrument, the strings of which were of gold and
silver.

Yet, notwithstanding that her Majesty was at this time in her

70 67th year [she was in fact 59] . . . and has thus borne the heavy
burden of ruling a kingdom 34 years, she need not indeed – to
judge both from her person and appearance – yield much to a
young girl of sixteen. She has a very dignified, serious and royal
look, and rules her kingdom with great discretion, in desirable
75 peace, felicity and in the fear of God. She has, by God's help and
assistance, known well how to meet her enemies hitherto: witness
that mighty Spanish Armada, which a few years ago was scattered
between Dover and Calais, and beaten by the English, an enemy
of inferior force compared with it. Hence she frequently uses their
80 motto: 'Si Deus pro nobis, quis contra nos?' [If God is for us, who
is against us? – *Romans* 8:31]. Which she also did on this occasion
when the discourse happened to turn upon that same Spanish
defeat.

> Jacob Rathgeb, Secretary to the Duke of Württemburg, in
> William Rye, *England as seen by foreigners in the days of
> Elizabeth and James I* (1967), pp 12–13

Questions

* *a* What are the various attitudes towards Elizabeth of Feria
(Section 1), Naunton, Hayward and Rathgeb (this section)? Do
they agree on anything?

* *b* What might have been Elizabeth's 'one act of stain or taint'
(extract *a*, line 9)?

c Naunton's attitude to Elizabeth and 'faction' is coloured by his
attitude to Stuart practice. What are the virtues and weaknesses
of Elizabeth's style of rule by 'faction' as he describes it?

* *d* Suggest specific ways in which Hayward's description of
Elizabeth is inaccurate or inordinately flattering.

* *e* What features of a 'Renaissance prince' do Naunton, Hayward
and Rathgeb identify?

3 From Queen to King

1603: When I came to court I found the Queen ill disposed, and
she kept her inner lodging; yet she, hearing of my arrival, sent for
me. I found her in one of her withdrawing chambers, sitting low
upon her cushions. She called me to her. I kissed her hand, and
5 told how it was my chiefest happiness to see her in safety and in
health, which I wished might long continue. She took me by the
hand, and wrung it hard, and said 'No, Robin, I am not well', and
then discoursed with me of her indisposition, and that her heart
had been sad and heavy for ten or twelve days, and in her
10 discourse she fetched not so few as forty or fifty great sighs. I was
grieved at the first to see her in this plight, for in all my lifetime

before I never knew her fetch a sigh, but when the Queen of Scots was beheaded. . . .

15 From that day forwards, she grew worse and worse. She remained upon her cushions four days and nights at the least. All about her could not persuade her either to take any sustenance or go to bed.

20 I, hearing that neither the physicians, nor none about her, could persuade her to take any course for her safety, feared her death would soon after ensue. I could not but think in what a wretched estate I should be left, most of my livelihood depending on her life. And hereupon I bethought myself with what grace and favour I was ever received by the King of Scots, whensoever I was sent to him. I did assure myself it was neither unjust nor unhonest

25 for me to do for myself, if God at that time should call her to His mercy. Hereupon I wrote to the King of Scots (knowing him to be the right heir to the crown of England) and certified him in what state her Majesty was. I desired him not to stir from Edinburgh: if of that sickness she should die, I would be the first

30 man that should bring him news of it. . . .

. . . Between one and two of the clock on Thursday morning [24 March 1603], he that I left in the cofferer's chamber brought me word the Queen was dead. . . . [Carey's departure for Scotland is delayed some hours by disagreements between court factions.] I

35 returned and took horse between nine and ten o'clock, and that night rode to Doncaster. The Friday night I came to my own house at Widdrington [Northumberland] . . . . Very early on Saturday I took horse for Edinburgh, and came to Norham [on the border] about twelve at noon, so that I might well have been

40 with the King at supper time, but I got a great fall by the way, and my horse with one of his heels gave me a great blow on the head that made me shed much blood. It made me so weak that I was forced to ride a soft pace after, so that the King was newly gone to bed by the time that I knocked at the gate. I was quickly let in,

45 and carried up to the King's chamber. I kneeled by him, and saluted him by his title of England, Scotland, France and Ireland. He gave me his hand to kiss, and bade me welcome. . . .

The Memoirs of Robert Carey, ed. F. H. Mares (1972), pp 57–63

Questions

a How had Elizabeth and James, each in their own ways, prepared for the succession?

b What kinds of people might not have shared Carey's eagerness to notify James promptly of Elizabeth's death?

c In what ways does Carey reassure himself and the reader of the legitimacy of his communication with James?

4 King Philip II Expresses his Goodwill

Madam,

I do not write very often to your Highness, knowing that the Count of Feria always gives account to you of all that is happening: I am only doing so now because I am impelled by the great wish
5 and anxiety I have to see the affairs of your Highness as well arranged and established as my own (as in effect I hold them to be) so that when the Count hands these to you he can tell you that I am occupied by them, and that it is well to see to them in time. I much beg your Highness to have faith in him just as much as you
10 would in me, and to look upon this as a matter which concerns nothing less than the preservation and security of your kingdom, and most certainly your Highness in this and in no matter what other affair which concerns you will find me always as true and good a brother as I have been in the past; and this will be told to
15 you by the Count to whom in all this I entrust myself so as not to weary with a lengthy letter your Highness whose serene person and royal estate may our Lord guard and prosper as I desire.

From Brussels, 29 April 1559.

E. M. Tenison, *Elizabethan England*, vol I, (pub. for the author, Leamington, 1933), illustration no 42

Questions

a   By his own account, what friendly interests did Philip have in Elizabeth and England?
★   b   What is the significance of the words 'as I have been in the past' (line 14)? (See Section 1, extract *b*, lines 64–70.)
★   c   What were Philip's motives and preoccupations in respect of England in 1559? How and why did these change in subsequent years?

5 Faction: Leicester and Sussex

. . . I do dissent from the common and received opinion that my Lord of Leicester was absolute and alone in her grace: . . . .

He was a very goodly person, tall and singularly well featured, and all his youth well favoured, of a sweet aspect, but high
5 foreheaded . . . .

Being thus in her grace, she called to mind the sufferings of his ancestors, both in her father's and sister's reigns, and restored his and his brother's blood, creating Ambrose, the elder, Earl of Warwick, and himself Earl of Leicester; and as he was . . . 'of her
10 first choice', so he rested not there, but long enjoyed her favour . . . .

I am not bound to give credit to all vulgar relations, or the libels

of his time, which are commonly forced and falsified suitable to
the words and humours of men in passion and discontent, but
15 what binds me to think him no good man, amongst other things
of known truth, is that [matter] of my Lord of Essex's death in
Ireland, and the marriage of his Lady [Leicester had married the
widow of the 1st Earl of Essex and mother of the 'famous' Earl];
which I forbear to press, in regard he is long since dead, and
20 others are living whom it may concern . . . .

. . . He was sent governor by the Queen to the revolted States
of Holland, where we read not of his wonders, for they say, he
had more of Mercury than of Mars . . . .

His co-rival was Thomas Radcliffe, Earl of Sussex, who in his
25 constellation was his direct opposite, for indeed he was one of the
Queen's martialists, and did her very good service in Ireland, at
her first accession, till she recalled him to the court, whom she
made Lord Chamberlain, but he played not his game with that
cunning and dexterity as the Earl of Leicester did, who was much
30 the fairer courtier, though Sussex was thought much the honester
man, and far the better soldier, but he lay too open on his guard;
he was a godly gentleman, and of a brave and noble nature, true
and constant to his friends and servants; he was also of a very
ancient and noble lineage, honoured through many descents,
35 through the title of Fitzwalters, . . . and to conclude this favourite,
it is confidently affirmed, that, lying in his last sickness, he gave
this caveat to his friends:

'I am now passing into another world, and I must leave you to
your fortunes, and the Queen's grace and goodness, but beware of
40 the gipsy (meaning Leicester), for he will be too hard for you all:
you know not the beast so well as I do.'

Sir Robert Naunton, op cit, pp 82, 99–103

Questions

a In which lines does Naunton hint that Leicester is open to
criticisms other than those he himself makes?

b How do you interpret Naunton's cryptic assessment of Leicester
as governor (lines 21–23)?

c What, in Naunton's eyes, were Sussex's qualities?

★ d In what ways might Elizabeth be thought to have benefited,
and in what ways suffered, from 'faction' among her chief
courtiers?

6 Cecil: Father and Son

William Cecil

He stood not by the way of constellation [fame], but was wholly
attentive to the service of his mistress, and his dexterity, experience

and merit therein challenged a room in the Queen's favour, which
5   eclipsed the others' over-seeming greatness . . . .
    . . . [At Elizabeth's accession] he was admitted Secretary of State;
afterwards he was made Master of the Court of Wards, then Lord
Treasurer, for he was a person of most excellent abilities; and
indeed the Queen began to need and seek out men of both guards
10 . . . for he had not to do with the sword more than as the great
paymaster and contriver of the war which shortly followed,
wherein he accomplished much, through his theoretical knowledge
at home and his intelligence abroad, by unlocking of the councils
of the Queen's enemies . . . .

15 *Robert Cecil*
    . . . he was first Secretary of State, then Master of the Court of
Wards, and, in the last year of her reign, came to be Lord
Treasurer, all of which were the steps of his father's greatness, and
of the honour he left to his house. For his person, he was not
20 much beholden to Nature, though somewhat for his face, which
was the best part of his outside: for his inside, it may be said, and
without offence, that he was his father's own son . . . he was a
courtier from his cradle . . . .
    He lived in those times wherein the Queen had most need and
25 use of men of weight, and amongst many able ones this was the
chief, as having taken his sufficiency from his instruction who
begat him, the tutorship of the times and court, which were then
academies of Art and Cunning. . . .
            Sir Robert Naunton, op cit, pp 103–4, 144–5

Questions

★   a   In what ways did William Cecil's early life differ from that of
        his son?
    b   Explain the phrase, 'unlocking of the councils of the Queen's
        enemies' (lines 13–14).
    c   What is Naunton's overall tone and attitude towards the
        Cecils?
    d   How does Naunton apportion credit for Robert Cecil's talents
        to Robert himself and to his father?
★   e   Comment on the phrase, 'the Queen had most need and use of
        men of weight' (lines 24–25).

7   A Spanish View of Drake

Testimony of Francisco de Zarate, taken prisoner by Francis
Drake off Guatemala, 4 April, 1579. To the Viceroy of New
Spain. [Original in Spanish.]

This general of the Englishmen is a nephew of John Hawkins,
5   and is the same who about five years ago [1572] took the port of
Nombre de Dios. He is called Francisco Drac, and is a man about
35 years of age [he was probably 38 or 39], low of stature, with a
fair beard, and is one of the greatest mariners that sails the seas,
both as a navigator and as a commander. His vessel is a galleon of
10   nearly 400 tons, and sails perfectly. She is manned with a hundred
men, all of service, and of an age for warfare, and all are as
practised therein as old soldiers from Italy could be. Each one
takes particular pains to keep his arquebus clean. He treats them
with affection, and they treat him with respect. He carries with
15   him nine or ten cavaliers, younger sons of English noblemen.
These form a part of his council which he calls together for even
the most trivial matter, although he takes advice from no one. But
he enjoys hearing what they say and afterwards issues his orders.
He has no favourite.
20   The aforesaid gentlemen sit at his table, as well as a Portuguese
pilot [Nuno da Silva, taken prisoner near Cape Verde], who spoke
not a word during all the time I was on board. He is served on
silver dishes with gold borders and gilded garlands in which are
his arms. He carries all possible dainties and perfumed waters. He
25   said that many of these had been given him by the Queen.
None of these gentlemen took a seat or covered his head before
him until he repeatedly urged him to do so. This galleon of his
carries about thirty heavy pieces of artillery and a great quantity of
firearms with the requisite ammunition and lead. He dines and
30   sups to the music of viols. He carries trained carpenters and
artisans, so as to be able to careen the ship [overhaul it on dry
land] at any time. Beside being new, the ship has a double lining. I
understand that all the men he carries with him receive wages,
because, when our ship was sacked, no man dared take anything
35   without his orders. He shows them great favour, but punishes the
least fault. He also carries painters who paint for him pictures of
the coast in its exact colours. This I was most grieved to see, for
each thing is so naturally depicted that no one who guides himself
according to these paintings can possibly go astray. . . .
40   This Corsair, like a pioneer, arrived two months before he
intended to pass through [the Strait of Magellan] and during that
time for many days there were great storms. So it was that one of
the gentlemen whom he had with him [Thomas Doughty] said to
him, 'we have been a long while in this strait, and you have placed
45   all of us who follow or serve you in danger of death. It would
therefore be prudent for you to give order that we return to the
North [Atlantic] Sea. . . .'
This gentleman must have sustained this opinion with more
vigour than appeared proper to the General. His answer was that
50   he had the gentleman carried below deck and put in irons. On

another day, at the same hour, he ordered him to be taken out and to be beheaded in the presence of all. The term of his imprisonment was no more than was necessary to substantiate the lawsuit that was conducted against him. All this he told me, speaking much
55 good about the dead man, but adding that he had not been able to act otherwise, because this was what the Queen's Service demanded. . . .

I managed to ascertain whether the general was well liked, and all said that they adored him . . . .

New Light on Drake, trans. Zelia Nuttall (Hakluyt Society, second series, vol 34, 1914), pp 206–9

Questions

a Analyse the ingredients of Drake's success under the headings of (i) prior preparations, (ii) good practice on the voyage, (iii) firm captainship, (iv) fair captainship.
★ b What was the outcome of this particular expedition?

8 Restless Essex

(a) The beginning of the Spring [1587] . . . Sluys was besieged, and my Lord of Essex stole from court with intent to get into Sluys, if he could; the Queen sent me after him, commanding me
5 to use the best means, if I could find him, to persuade him to return to court. I made no long stay, but with all the speed I could, went after him: I found him at Sandwich, and with much ado I got him to return . . . .

[In 1589 was] the Journey of Portugal, where my Lord of Essex stole from court to go that journey [*sic*], and left me behind him,
10 which did so much trouble me, that I had no mind to stay in the court . . . .

The Memoirs of Robert Carey, op cit, pp 5,11

(b) Earl of Essex to Sir Henry Upton [July 1595?]

. . . This week I am not my own man. In the beginning of the next the Queen removes; but if you will then be privately at
15 London, towards the end of the week, I will appoint a place and time of meeting with you.

Earl of Essex to the Queen [1595?]

. . . the sad and grievous remembrance of these late months past and my restless desire to enjoy better times with your Majesty
20 do move me, nay force me, to set pen to paper. And yet, if it were question only of my own sufferings . . . I should have cloaked my passions, as I have done often when my health has been impaired and my mind weighed down. But as the two ends

of my life have been, the one to please you, the other to serve
25   you, I have found many, yea most times of late that instead of
being a contentment and entertainment to your Majesty's mind I
have been a distaste and disquiet. . . .

    Earl of Essex to Earl of Southampton [1599]

    March 6th. The Queen and I have had no jar since I came. Of
30   you nor of any particular friend of mine or place in the army,
there has been no mention: which I was content to let pass because
when my commission is once past it will give me authority in
direct words to bestow all places, and then if she quarrel with me,
her wrong is the greater and my standing upon it will appear
35   more just. . . .

                Calendar of the MSS of the Marquis of Salisbury, vol XIII,
                pp 537, 549 and vol XIV, Addenda, p 107

Questions

a   What were Essex's faults in the eyes of the queen, as presented
      in these extracts?

b   What are the meaning and significance of the phrase, 'to
      bestow all places' (line 33)?

★ *c*   Comparing these extracts with Chapter V, Section 5, and
         Chapter VII, Section 4*b*, and with your wider reading, account
         for Essex's ultimate fate.

★ *d*   Comment on the 'final resting place' of the letters in extract *b*
         (that is, the collection of papers to which they found their
         way). Do this, and the letters themselves, provide us with any
         clues about the workings of 'faction' in Elizabethan England?

9   English and Irish Views of Shane O'Neill

(a) *The English view*

1562: Now was come Shane O'Neill out of Ireland, to perform
what he had promised a year before, with a guard of axe-bearing
gallowglasses, bareheaded, with curled hair hanging down, yellow
surplices dyed with saffron . . . long sleeves, short coats and hairy
5   mantles, whom the English people gazed at with no less admiration
than nowadays [early 17th Century] they do them of China and
America. He being received with all kindness, and falling down at
the Queen's feet, confessed his crime and rebellion with howling,
and obtained pardon. Being gently asked by what right he had
10   excluded Hugh, his brother Matthew's son, out of his inheritance,
he answered fiercely (as he had done before already in Ireland): by
very good right, to wit, that he [Shane] being certain and lawful son
and heir of Con, as born of his lawful wife, had entered upon his
father's inheritance; that Matthew was the son of a blacksmith of

15 Dundalk . . . born after [Con's] marriage with his wife Alison, but
by his mother cunningly obtruded upon Con for his son. . . .

For his part he was by the law of God and Man the certain heir
. . . and by joint consent of the nobility and people, designed
'O'Neill', according to the law of that country, called Tanistry, by
20 which a man of ripe age is to be preferred before a child, and the
Uncle before the nephew. . . .

. . . He was sent home again with honour, and for a while
performed stout and faithful service against the Hebridean
rovers. . . .

25 1567 [after many campaigns against the English], Shane, taking
heart again, harried the country round about, besieged Dundalk
again, which siege he was fain shortly after to break up again with
great loss and shame. . . . He himself, when he saw his companies
weakened, . . . the passages beset, and all refuges seized on by the
30 English was minded to cast himself at the Lord Deputy's feet with
a halter about his neck, and crave pardon. But his secretary
dissuaded him, advising him first to try the friendship of the
Hebridean Scots, who during the heat of the war had returned
into Clandeboy [County Antrim]. . . . They, in revenge of their
35 brethren and kinsmen whom he had slain received him with
feigned courtesy, and soon after, taking him into their tent,
amongst their cups, they fell to hot words . . . drew upon him,
and slew him and most of his company.

This bloody end had Shane in the middle of June, who had
40 despoiled his father of the government, and his base brother of his
life: a man most polluted with murders and adulteries, a very
great rioter and glutton, and such a drunkard that to cool his body
when it was immoderately inflamed with wine and whiskey, he
would many times be buried in the earth up to his chin. . . .

William Camden, *The History of the Most Renowned and
Victorious Princess Elizabeth* (1630), pp 61–2, 105–6

(b) The Irish view

[Original in Erse.]
45 . . . And the reception he got [from the Scots of Clandeboy],
after having been some time in their company . . . was to mangle
him nimbly, and put him unsparingly to the sword, and bereave
him of life. Grievous to the race of Owen, son of Neill, was the
death of him who was there slain. For that O'Neill, i.e. John
50 [Shane], had been their Conchebhar in provincial dignity, their
Lugh Longhanded in heroism [ancient Irish heroes] and their
champion in danger and prowess.

Annals of the Kingdom of Ireland, by the Four Masters ed.
J. O'Donovan (1854, reprinted A. M. S. Press Inc., 1966), vol
V, pp 1619–23

Questions

a   What interest had Elizabeth in pardoning and recognising O'Neill?

b   What evidence in extract *a* suggests that O'Neill's secretary's advice was bad, apart from its outcome?

★ c   What reasons can you suggest for the Irish Law of succession by 'tanistry'? Does extract *b* support your suggestions?

d   Do the extracts shed any light on English perceptions of the Irish, and on Irish perceptions of themselves?

10   An Exercise in Character Assassination: the Death of Christopher Marlowe

(a) Not inferior to any of the former in Atheism and impiety, and equal to all in manner of punishment was one of our own nation, of fresh and late memory, called Marlin [Marlowe], by profession a scholar, brought up from his youth in the University of
5   Cambridge, but by practice a playmaker, and a poet of scurrility, who by giving too large a swing to his own wit, and suffering his lust to have the full reins, fell (not without just desert) to that outrage and extremity that he denied God and His Son Christ, and not only in word blasphemed the Trinity, but also (as it is credibly
10 reported) wrote books against it, affirming our Saviour to be but a deceiver, and Moses to be but a conjurer and seducer of the people, and the Holy Bible to be but vain and idle stories, and all religion but a device of policy. But see what a hook the Lord put in the nostrils of this barking dog: it so fell out, that in London
15 streets as he purposed to stab one whom he owed a grudge to with his dagger, the other party perceiving so avoided the stroke, that withal catching hold of his wrist, he stabbed his own dagger into his own head, in such sort that, notwithstanding all the means of surgery that could be wrought, he shortly after died
20 thereof. The manner of his death being so terrible (for he ever cursed and blasphemed to his last gasp, and together with his breath an oath flew out of his mouth) that it was not only a manifest sign of God's judgment, but also an horrible and fearful terror to all that beheld him. . . .

> Thomas Beard, *Theatre of God's Judgments*, Chapter XXV (1597), in J. L. Hotson, *The Death of Christopher Marlow* (1925), p 11

25 (b) . . . Inquisition [inquest] . . . taken at Deptford Strand in the aforesaid County of Kent within the verge [area of jurisdiction of the court?] on the first day of June in the year of the reign of Elizabeth . . . thirty-fifth [1593] . . . upon view of the body of

30 Christopher Morley [Marlowe], there lying dead and slain, upon oath of . . . [16 names], who say [upon] their oath that when a certain Ingram Ffrysar [Frizer] . . . and the aforesaid Christopher Morley and one Nicholas Skeres . . . and Robert Poley . . . on the 30th day of May . . . at Deptford Strand . . . about the tenth hour before noon of the same day, met together in a room in the house
35 of a certain Eleanor Bull, widow . . . and after supper the said Ingram and Christopher Morley were in speech and uttered one to the other diverse malicious words for the reason that they could not be at one nor agree about the payment of the sum of pence, that is, the reckoning there; . . . it so befell that the said
40 Christopher Morley on a sudden and of his malice towards the said Ingram aforesaid, then and there maliciously drew the dagger of the said Ingram which was at his back, and with the same dagger the said Christopher Morley then and there maliciously gave the aforesaid Ingram two wounds on his head of the length of two
45 inches and of the depth of a quarter of an inch; whereupon the said Ingram, in fear of being slain . . . in his own defence and for the saving of his life, then and there struggled with the said Christopher Morley to get back from him his dagger aforesaid . . . and so it befell in that affray that the said Ingram in defence of
50 his life, with the dagger aforesaid of the value of twelve pence, gave the said Christopher then and there a mortal wound over his right eye of the depth of two inches and of the width of one inch; of which mortal wound the aforesaid Christopher Morley then and there instantly died.

J. L. Hotson, op cit, pp 31–3

Questions

a   In what factual details of Marlowe's death do extracts *a* and *b* differ?
b   At face value, which account is more authentic?
c   What is the purpose of Beard's tract?
d   What is the Inquest at pains to prove about Marlowe and about Frizer?
★ e   It has been suggested that Marlow's murder was approved by government agents. Do the extracts, or your further study, lend any support to this proposition?

II 'Windows into Men's Hearts' – Religion

Introduction

Young school students have sometimes drawn diagrams of the 'swing of the pendulum' between Protestantism and Catholicism in Tudor England; the break with Rome under Henry, further towards Protestantism under Edward, back to Catholicism under Mary and 'finally' to the Protestant Elizabethan settlement. But what do these oscillations represent? Royal will? The surge and retreat of theological arguments? Changes in the public mood in religion?

Certainly the 'settlement' of 1558–59 was not final and in Elizabeth's reign there was 'all to play for'. What of the queen – was she urging the Commons on or attempting to restrain them? What was her subsequent attitude to the bishops and to Puritan and Catholic dissent? Does Elizabeth deserve her reputation for 'moderation' in religion, or did the persecution of active dissent reach a climax as bloody under her as under her sister Mary?

What of parliament? Was it religious temper as easily identified as some historians have professed? Was not religion, in fact, possibly just one more weapon in the battle for privilege? Henry VIII had actively encouraged parliamentary participation in religious change – now Elizabeth often sought to ban religious debate. What of the Puritan preachers and Catholic priests – recusant, seminary and Jesuit? Are they indeed 'poles apart' or do they rather resemble each other in their mixture of aggressive missionary zeal and pious self-criticism, their minority status, their foreign inspirations and their responses to persecution?

The religious attitude of the people at large is the hardest thing to fathom, as contemporary religious enthusiasts, Puritan, Anglican and Catholic alike, discovered. The common mind in religion is faintly recorded, although many diocesan and parish records have been published by county and district record societies and they reveal the uphill task which the established church had in influencing the minds of English people, often crypto-Catholic, conservative or downright anti-clerical and profane.

Perhaps this cleavage between religious activists of all colours and the secular majority is the most significant division of all.

Perhaps, too, all categorisation is vain, and we should believe that many Elizabethans would have echoed the words of Fulke Greville;

'Yet when each of us, in his own heart looks,
He finds the God there, far unlike his books'.

1 A New Establishment

(a) The Act of Supremacy

. . . To the intent that all usurped and foreign power and authority spiritual and temporal may for ever be clearly extinguished and never to be [sic] used nor obeyed within this realm or any other your Majesty's dominions or countries: may it please your
5   Highness that it may be further enacted, by the authority aforesaid, that no foreign prince, person, prelate, state or potentate spiritual or temporal shall at any time after the last day of this session of parliament use, enjoy or exercise any manner of power, jurisdiction, superiority, authority, pre-eminence or privilege spiritual or
10 ecclesiastical within this realm. . . .

1 Elizabeth c.1 (1559), *Statutes of the Realm*, vol IV, Part 1, p 352

(b) The Act of Uniformity

. . . From and after the said feast of the Nativity of St. John Baptist next coming [7 January], all and every person and persons inhabiting within this realm or any other the Queen's Majesty's dominions, shall diligently and faithfully, having no lawful or
15 reasonable excuse to be absent, endeavour themselves to resort to their parish church or chapel accustomed, or upon reasonable let thereof to some usual place where common prayer and such service of God shall be used in such time of let, upon every Sunday and other days ordained and used to be kept as holy days, and then
20 and there to abide orderly and soberly during the time of the common prayer, preachings or other service of God there to be used and ministered; upon pain of punishment by the censures of the church, and also upon pain that every person so offending shall forfeit for every such offence twelve pence, to be levied by
25 the churchwardens of the parish where such offence shall be done, to the use of the poor of the same parish, of the goods, lands and tenements of such offender by way of distress.

1 Elizabeth c.2 (1559), *Statutes of the Realm*, vol IV, Part 1, pp 356–7

a Why did the Act of Supremacy legislate against 'all usurped and foreign power and authority spiritual *or temporal*' (extract *a*, lines 6–7)?

★ b Trace the history of the title to supremacy in the English church, from the break with Rome to the title which Elizabeth bore.

★ c What many and varied reasons existed for non-attendance at parish churches early in Elizabeth's reign?

d How did the framers of the Act of Uniformity attempt to link the problems of conformity with that of poor relief?

★ e To what sum did the fine for recusancy rise in 1581?

★ f Where in parliament did the bills for supremacy and uniformity meet with the greatest degrees of resistance and support?

2 Reformation from Below

1558: Il Schifanoya to Ottaviano Vivaldino, Ambassador from Mantua to the Court of King Philip in Brussels. [original in Italian]

5 Until now I have believed that the matters of religion would continue in the accustomed manner, her Majesty having promised this with her own mouth many times; but now I have lost faith, and I see that by little and little they are returning to the [former] bad use. On Christmas Day the Bishop of Carlisle [Owen Oglethorpe] sang high mass, and her Majesty sent to tell

10 him that he was not to elevate the host; to which the good Bishop replied that thus had he learnt the mass, and that she must pardon him as he could not do otherwise; so, the Gospel being ended, her Majesty rose and departed, and on the other days it has been so done by her chaplains.

15 On the same day, in the church of St. Augustine, assigned to the Italian nation, two individuals (whom I will not call preachers, for they were mechanics and cobblers), followed by a very great mob, entered by force, breaking the locks of the doors. Both of them leaped into the pulpit and, book in hand, commenced

20 reading and preaching to the people one following the other, uttering a thousand ribaldries concerning the reign of the blessed memory of Queen Mary and of the Cardinal [Pole], and vituperating the people for the errors they had committed in believing their former teachers; so that never was there seen a finer

25 metamorphosis than two rogues at once preaching in the same pulpit.

This took place in the morning, and in the afternoon they did the like in the Church of St. Anthony [St. Anthony's Hospital, Threadneedle Street?], which heretofore was assigned to the

30 French nation, and also on St. Stephen's Day [26 December].
They meant to continue their practices on the other holy days, but
were given to understand by the Queen that neither they nor
any other persons were any longer to preach, for fear of greater
scandal or of some insurrection, as many disputes and controversies
35 had already taken place. . . .

Calendar of State Papers Venetian, vol VII (1558–1580), p 2

Questions

a   To what period was the writer referring as the time of 'the
    (former) bad use' (lines 6–7)?
b   From the evidence of the extract, to what extent did the queen
    deter, and to what extent encourage, the kind of Protestant
    demonstration reported here?
c   What motives other than religious may have prompted the
    invasions of these two London churches?
★ d   Why were Queen Mary and Cardinal Pole the objects of such
    strong verbal abuse so soon after their deaths?

3   The Established Church at Work

Bishop Barnes's Injunctions for Durham diocese 1577

1.   First, we monish and straitly [strictly] enjoin and command
that all and singular the Queen's Majesty['s] Injunctions be in all
respects duly and faithfully observed, performed and fulfilled. . . .
2.   Item, that the parsons, vicars and curates and churchwardens
5 do within their several parishes take order and see that the Blessed
Sacrament of the Body and Blood of our Saviour Jesu Christ be
reverently ministered and received in every parish church at least
once every month; and that they see and diligently look that all
and every their parishioners being above fourteen years of age do
10 openly receive the Holy Communion in their parish church at the
least twice every year, whereof at the feast of Easter to be
once. . . .
3.   Item, that no notorious adulterer, fornicator, incestuous
person, filthy and common drunkard, horrible swearers or
15 blasphemers of the name of God, curser or banner or beater of
father or mother, or known usurer, or any other notorious evil
liver, be admitted to the Holy Communion before they shall first
be reconverted, reconciled or punished. . . .
4.   Item, we monish and straitly charge that none be admitted to
20 the Holy Communion which are not confirmed and which cannot
say the Catechism perfectly. . . .
5.   Item, that no Communions or Commemorations (as some
call them) be said for the dead, or at the burials of the dead. . . .

25 6.   Item, that no popish abrogated Holy-days be kept holily, nor
any Divine Service publicly said or celebrated on any such days;
nor any superfluous fast be used as those called the Lady fast, or
St. Trinyon's fast [St. Ninian's], the Black-fast, St. Margaret's fast
or such other, invented by the devil to the dishonouring of God
30 and damnation of the souls of idolatrous and superstitious people.
    7.   Item, that no rites or ceremonies be used at the ministration of
the Sacraments and celebration of Divine Service, other than are
expressed, set down and prescribed in the Book of Common
Prayer . . . and that the parsons, vicars and curates at ministration
35 of sacraments wear clean and comely surplices; and that they
abroad do wear clerkly and decent apparel, as gowns or cloaks
with sleeves of sad colour, and none unseemly apparel, as great
ruffs, great breeches, gascon hose, scaling, nor any other like
monstrous and unseemly apparel, only round cloaks when they
40 ride to cast off the mire and dust may be used, but not otherwise.
    8.   Item, that no midwives, nor any other women, be suffered to
minister baptism; but if the infants be weak and the parents
likewise, that they cannot expect the Sabbath day, that the minister
or some other godly and discreet person . . . do baptise such
45 infants at home. . . .
    9.   Item, that no parsons, vicars, curates or other persons
ecclesiastical, being unmarried, do hereafter retain or keep any
women in his or their houses other than such as are allowed by the
Injunctions; nor that any of them do haunt or frequent any
50 common taverns or alehouses, or any unlawful games, as carding,
dicing, bowling, dancing or such like, or any fencing schools,
May games; nor that any of their mansion houses be kept as
alehouses, taverns or houses of gaming and such evil rule. . . .

W. P. M. Kennedy, *Elizabethan Episcopal Administration*
(Alcuin Book Collections XXV and XXVII, 1924), vol II,
pp 70–3

Questions

a   Which statute was Injunction 2 reinforcing?
b   Which injunctions were intended to defend the fabric of society
      in general?
c   Which injunctions were directed against Roman Catholicism?
★ *d* Assuming that rules are made because the things ruled against
      are common abuses, describe the state of the Church at parish
      level in Elizabeth's reign, using the extract and any other
      evidence you have.

4 Edmund Grindal, the Puritans and the Queen

(a) Grindal and the Puritans

The Examination of certain Londoners before the Ecclesiastical Commissioners, 20 June 1567.

Bishop Grindal [of London] . . . In this severing yourselves from the society of other Christians, you condemn not only us,
5 but also the whole state of the church reformed in King Edward's days, which was well reformed according to the word of God, yea, and many good men have shed their blood for the same, which your doings condemn.

Robert Hawkins: We condemn them not, in that we stand to the
10 truth of God's word . . . .

Bishop Grindal: But have you not the gospel truly preached, and the sacraments ministered accordingly, and good order kept, although we differ from other churches in ceremonies, and in indifferent things, which lie in the prince's power to command for
15 order's sake? How say you, Smith? You seem to be the ancientest of them; answer you.

John Smith: Indeed, my Lord, we thank God for reformation and that is it we desire, according to God's word . . . .

William White: I beseech you, let me answer.
20 *Bishop Grindal:* Nay, William White, hold your peace; you shall be heard anon.

William Nixon: I beseech you, let me answer a word or two.

Bishop Grindal: Nixon, you are a busy fellow. I know your words; you are full of talk. I know from whence you came.
25 *Robert Hawkins:* I would be glad to answer.

Bishop Grindal: Smith shall answer. Answer you, Smith.

John Smith: Indeed, as you said even now, for preaching and ministering the sacraments, so long as we might have the word freely preached, and the sacraments administered without the
30 preferring of idolatrous gear above it, we [would have] never assembled together in houses. But when it came to this point, that all our preachers were displaced by your Law, so that we could not hear none of them in any church by the space of seven or eight weeks, except Father Coverdale, of whom we have a good
35 opinion; and yet (God knows) the man was so fearful, that he durst not be known unto us where he preached, though we sought it at his house. And then were we troubled and commanded to your courts from day to day, for not coming to our parish churches. Then we bethought us what were best to do; and we
40 remembered that there was a congregation of us in this city in Queen Mary's days: and a congregation at Geneva, which used a book and order of preaching, ministering of the sacraments and discipline, most agreeable to the word of God; which book is

allowed by that godly and well learned man, Master Calvin, and
45 the preachers there; which book and order we now hold. And if
you can reprove this book, or anything that we hold, by the word
of God, we will yield to you, and do open penance at Paul's
Cross: if not, we will stand to it by the grace of God.

Bishop Grindal: This is no answer.

50 *William White:* You may be answered, if you will give leave.

Bishop Grindal: White, you shall speak anon: let the elder speak
first.

John Smith: Would you have me go back from the better, to
such churches that I had leave go to mass as go to them, they are
55 so evil favouredly used; as the parish church where I dwell is one.
He is a very papist that is there, and yet he has another place too.

Dean Goodman: Lo, he counts the service and reformation in
King Edward's days as evil as the mass.

Bishop Grindal: Lo, because he knows one that is evil, he finds
60 fault with all. But you may go to other places, as at St. Laurence.

William White: You say we find fault with all, for one papist. If
it were well tried, there should a great company of papists be
found in this city, whom you do allow to be preachers and
ministers, and thrust out the godly for your pleasure's sake . . .

      Puritanism in Tudor England, ed. H. C. Porter (1970),
      pp 81–3

(b) Grindal and the Queen

65 [20 December 1576: Edmund Grindal (now Archbishop of
Canterbury) to the Queen.]

With most humble remembrance of my bounden duty to your
Majesty, it may please the same to be advertised that the speeches
which it has pleased you to deliver to me, when I last attended on
70 your Highness, concerning abridging the number of preachers,
and the utter suppression of all learned exercises and conferences
among the ministers of the church, allowed by their bishops and
ordinaries, have exceedingly dismayed and discomforted me. Not
so much for that the said speeches sounded very hardly against
75 mine own person being but one particular man, and not much to
be accounted of: but most of all for that the same might both tend
to the public harm of God's church, whereof your Highness ought
by office to be 'nurse', and also to the heavy burdening of your
own conscience before God, if they should be put in strict
80 execution. It was not your Majesty's pleasure then, the time not
serving thereto, to hear me at any length concerning the said two
matters then propounded; I thought it therefore my duty by
writing to declare some part of my mind unto your Highness:
beseeching the same with patience to read over this that I now
85 send, written with mine own rude scribbling hand, which seems

to be of more length that it is indeed, for I say with Ambrose, 'I
write with mine own hand, for you alone to read it'.

And so to come to the present case: . . . . I cannot marvel
enough how this strange opinion should once enter into your
90 mind that it should be good for the Church to have few preachers.
Alas, Madam, is the scripture any more plain in any one thing,
than that the gospel of Christ should be plentifully preached? . . .

Now for the second point, which is concerning the learned
exercise and conference amongst the ministers of the Church: I
95 have consulted with diverse of my brethren the bishops by letters,
who think the same as I do: a thing most profitable to the Church,
and therefore expedient to be continued . . . .

. . . And now being sorry that I have been so long and tedious
to your Majesty, I will draw to an end, most humbly praying the
100 same well to consider these two short petitions following.

The first is, that you would refer all these ecclesiastical matters
which touch religion, or the doctrine and discipline of the Church,
to the bishops of divines of your realm, according to the example
of all godly Christian emperors and princes of all ages . . . .

105 The second petition I have to make to your Majesty is this: that
when you deal in matters of faith and religion, or matters that
touch the Church of Christ, which is His spouse, brought with so
dear a price, you would not use to pronounce so resolutely and
peremptorily, *as from authority*, as you may do in civil and
110 extern[al] matters; but always remember that in God's causes the
will of God, and not the will of any earthly creatures, is to take
place. . . .

> B. M. Lans. Ms. 23.12, in Claire Cross, *the Royal Supremacy
> in the Elizabethan Church* (1969), pp 171–3

Questions

  a Given that extract *a* was a record made by the examinees, what
degree of bias do you detect in it?

  b What device of questioning does Grindal apparently use to
muzzle the more articulate prisoners?

★ *c* What does Grindal mean by 'indifferent things' (extract *a*,
line 14)? Give examples of points of disagreement between the
established church and 'Puritans' in these 'indifferent things'.

  d What pressures had been put on these prisoners and their
associates to attend parish churches and not assemble in private
houses?

★ *e* According to the opposing parties in extract *a*, what were the
foundations of 'authority' in religion?

  f From the evidence of extract *b* (lines 80–87) what had the
atmosphere of the previous conversation been, and what
manner does Grindal seem to want to adopt in this letter?

★   g   How had the matter of 'prophesyings', or 'exercises and conferences', developed up to the date of extract *b*?

★   h   What happened because of this letter (extract *b*)?

     i   From the evidence of these two extracts, comment on the position of Grindal as 'piggy in the middle'. How well does he acquit himself?

5   The Puritan mind

(a) *Diary of Richard Rogers, 18 August 1587*

We complain that many things are amiss in our lives, but we can see no cause of it. And this is a very common thing with good men, that when they come to have dealings, occupyings [occupations] and families much of their delight is employed upon
5   them which was wont to be given to the Lord, and yet all was thought to be too little. And the Apostle [Paul] in *I Cor[inthians]* 7, has taught us that as single men bestow all their care how they may please the Lord, so the married have commonly their care without especial grace how they may grow on together and
10   prosper, by means whereof much coldness and neglig[ence] grows upon them before they be aware. Besides we may observe by exper[ience] that even the most zealous do somewhat in time decline and wax remiss in caring for the matter of God. So that no prayer may be more meet for a good Christian than this, that God
15   would keep us in our age from the corruption of the time and of the world. For full soon a man falls to be like others, and there is great force and strength in the times and persons with whom we live. When we enjoy our peace, liberty and other commod[ities] upon such conditions as the times do oft[en] offer us, it is to be
20   feared that we yield to somewhat that we should not – for mine own part I see cause to fear this in myself, and I hope I will look more diligently to myself than I have done and wean myself from some lawful profits and pleasures, much more to make more consc[ience] of such as be unlawful, yea even of thoughts which
25   are with delight in things that ought not to be. And will wait what encouragement the Lord will give me.

          Two Elizabethan Puritan Diaries, ed. M. M. Knappen (1933), p 57

(b) *Samuel Ward's diary at Christ's College, Cambridge, 14 June 1595*

My negligence in not calling upon God before I went to Chapel, and the little desire I had there to call on God, and my drowsiness in God's service. My sins even through the whole day, being
30   Sunday: 1. My negligence aforesaid. 2. My hearing the sermon

without that sense which I should have had. 2 [*sic*] In not praying
God to bless it to me afterward. 3. In not talking of good things at
dinner. . . . 4. In the immoderate use of God's creatures. 5. In
sleeping immediately after dinner. 6. In not preparing me to
35 sermon till it tolled. 7. In sluggish hearing of God's word, and
that for my great dinner. 8. In hearing another sermon sluggishly.
9. In returning home and omitting our repetition of sermons by
reason that my countryman Ewbank was with me. 10. In not
exhorting him to any good thing. 11. In not going to evening
40 prayers. 12. In supping liberally, never remembering our poor
brethren. 13. In not taking order to give the poor women
somewhat at 7 o'clock. 14. My dullness in stirring of my brother
to Christian meditations. 15. My want of affections in hearing the
sermons repeated. 16. My sluggishness in prayer, and thus sin I
45 daily against three, O Lord. . . .
June 21st 1595. . . . My too much drinking after supper; my
idle talk with Tunstall of Durham matters. . . .
June 27th 1595. . . . My immoderate diet in eating cheese, very
hurtful for my body at 3 o'clock. . . .
50 July 12th 1595. . . . My negligence in fasting, whereas I
had purposed it. Also my over great mirth at afternoon,
notwithstanding I ought to have been sorry, both for the imminent
danger which was to befall our college [from the election of an
unworthy fellow], as also of the unseasonable weather which was
55 like to cause a dearth. . . .
September 16th 1595. . . . My forgetfullness to write to my
friends out of Cambridge, as to Mr. Allenson. No doubt they will
forget me when I am gone, and that justly. . . .
October 3rd 1595. . . . My immoderate eating of walnuts and
60 cheese after supper, whereby I did distemper my body. . . .
Two Elizabethan Puritan Diaries, ed. M. M. Knappen (1933),
pp 108–11

Questions

a What subjects for self-criticism do Richard Rogers and Samuel
Ward appear to have in common?

b Comment on lines 16–18 in extract *a*.

c For what reasons does Samuel Ward repent of eating too
much?

★ d Generalising from these extracts, and from your wider reading,
could you attempt a description of 'the Puritan mind'?

6　The Catholics

(a) Catholics driven underground

An inventory of such superstitious things as were found in Sir
John Southworth's hosue at Samlesbury [Lancashire], by Richard
Brereton, Esquire, one of her Majesty's Justices of the Peace, at a
search made there by the said Richard Brereton, Esquire, 21st
5　November in the 35th year of the reign of our Sovereign Lady
Elizabeth the Queen etc., 1592.

Imprimis: one canopy to hang over the altar, found in a secret
vault over the dining chamber and another chamber.

Item: two candlesticks of brass, of the fashion used in the time
10　of superstition found in the same place.

Item: fourteen images of diverse fashions, found in the same
vault. All which things were delivered to the Constable of
Samlesbury to deliver to my Lord's [Lord Lieutenant's?] honour.

Item: eleven books of papistry found in a chamber, delivered to
15　the said Constable to deliver to my Lord's honour.

Item: one head piece delivered to the said Constable to deliver to
my Lord's honour. All the rest of the armour is in the custody of
James Cooke of Preston, who has a yearly pension given him to
scour and keep fair the same.

20　Item: found in another chamber: thirteen books of papistry, that
is to say,

A Reims testament.

An apology of the English Seminaries.

A defence of the censure given upon two books written against
25　Edmund Campion, priest.

A treatise of Schism, showing that all Catholics must absent
themselves from heretical conventicles, to wit, prayer and
sermons.

A discovery of John Nichols. All the rest of the books are
30　written.

Item: found in the same chamber; one blue coat, with Sir John
Southworth's cognizance upon the same.

Item: a doublet and pair of hose.

Item: a frieze gown without a pocket, and yet devices secretly
35　to keep letters in, and certain other apparel; all which books and
apparel was reported to be the goods of one Edward Sager.

The answer of John Wright, servant to Sir John Southworth,
Knight:

John Wright, servant to Sir John Southworth, being examined,
40　says that there be dwelling and remaining in the house of the said
Sir John Southworth, called Samlesbury, these persons whose
names are underwritten [41 names are appended]. And this
examinate, being asked when he saw any Jesuit or seminary priest
in his master's house, says that he saw none there for the space of

45 five years last past; and for the space of fourteen years this examinate says that he saw no unknown person or stranger in his master's house.

> *The Egerton Papers*, ed. J. Payne Collier (Camden Society, 1840), pp 163–6

(b) Cardinal Allen's apologia

. . . Many priests and other Catholics in England have been persecuted, condemned and executed for mere matters of religion
50 and for transgression only of new statutes which do make cases of conscience to be treason without all pretence or surmise of any old treasons or statutes for the same.

. . . And herein to deal particularly and plainly, we allege the worthy priest and Bachelor of Divinity, Mr. Cuthbert Mayne
55 (who suffered a glorious martyrdom at Launceston in the province of Cornwall, for that the case or cover only of an 'Agnus Dei', and a printed copy of that bull, now expired, which denounced to the Christian world the last Jubilee [1574–5], were found about him), condemned not by any old laws (as is deceitfully pretended
60 to abuse the simple of our own nation and strangers that knew not our lamentable condition) but by a late statute enacted the thirteenth year of the Queen's reign [13 Elizabeth c.2.] which makes it high treason to bring from Rome any beads, sacred pictures, 'Agnus Deis', bulls or (as the express words of the statute
65 are) 'any writing or instrument, written or printed, containing any thing, matter or cause whatsoever', by which words they may condemn a man to death as guilty of high treason though he bring from Rome but letters testimonial for a traveller's credit and commendation in journey: a thing unheard of in all ages, not
70 credible to foreigners and a fable to the posterity, or rather a warning to the world to come, into what misery and barbarousness a kingdom that forsakes the Church may be brought into. And an honourable gentleman of an ancient family (Francis Tregian), for only receiving the said blessed priest into his house, remains
75 condemned at this day to perpetual prison and has lost both lands and goods of great importance for that fact.

> William (Cardinal) Allen, *A True, Sincere and Modest Defence of English Catholics*, ed. R. Kingdon (1965), pp 60–2

Questions

a   Give examples of items found at Samlesbury (extract *a*) which suggest the survival of Catholicism, and examples of items which suggest the work of English priests returning from abroad.

b   What is the significance of the reference to Reims in extract *a*, line 22?

★   c   What positive efforts to convert Catholics to Protestantism were attempted in Lancashire in Elizabeth's reign? (See Chapter VII, Section 3f, lines 59–67.)

       d   In what way, according to Allen (extract b), was Elizabeth's persecution of Catholics more unreasonable than prosecution of heresy and treason in previous reigns?

★   e   Explain how the Papal Bull of 1570 linked Catholicism with treason in the eyes of the English authorities.

       f   How did the English authorities respond to the Bull of 1570 (extract b, lines 61–69)?

(c) The Catholic Missionary

[Edmund Campion to Claude Aquaviva (General of the Society of Jesus), 17 November 1580.]

I ride about some piece of the country every day. The harvest is wonderful great. On horseback I meditate my sermon: when I
5   come to the house, I polish it. Then I talk with such as come to speak with me, or hear their confessions. In the morning, after Mass, I preach; they hear with exceeding greediness, and very often receive the Sacrament, for the ministration whereof we are ever well assisted by priests whom we find in every place whereby
10   both the people is well served, and we much eased in our charges.
. . . I cannot long escape the hands of the heretics; the enemies have so many eyes, so many tongues, so many scouts and crafts. I am in apparel myself very ridiculous: I often change it, and my name also. I read letters sometimes myself that in the first front
15   tell news that Campion is taken, which noised in every place where I come, so fills my ears with the sound thereof, that fear itself has taken away all fear. My soul is in mine own hands ever.
. . . Marry, the solaces that are ever intermingled with the miseries are so great, that they do not only countervail the fear of what
20   punishment temporal soever, but by infinite sweetness make all wordly pains, be they never so great, seem nothing. A conscience pure, a courage invincible, zeal incredible, a work so worthy the number innumerable, of high degree, of mean calling, of the inferior sort, of every age and sex.
25   Here, even amongst the Protestants themselves that are of milder nature, it is turned into a proverb that he must be a Catholic that pays faithfully what he owes, insomuch that if any Catholic do injury, everybody expostulates with him, as for an act unworthy of men of that calling. To be short, heresy hears ill of
30   all men; neither is there any condition of people commonly counted more vile and impure than their ministers, and we worthily have indignation that fellows so unlearned, so evil, so derided, so base, should in so desperate a quarrel overrule such a number of noble wits as our realm has. Threatening edicts come
35   forth against us daily; notwithstanding, by good heed, and the

prayers of good men, and which is the chief of all, God's special gift, we have passed safely through the most part of the island. I find many neglecting their own security to have only care of my safety.

> The Other Face, Catholic Life under Elizabeth I, ed. P. Caraman (1960), pp 114–15

(d) Internal and external dangers

40 [Henry Garnet, S. J., to Claude Aquaviva (General of the Society of Jesus) 16 April 1596 (original in Latin).]

Many months ago a certain priest [John Mush] had business at Rome and he set out thence on his return journey to England not long before the death of Cardinal [William] Allen. Whilst there,
45 this priest spread in the English College a report that the priests of Southern England (he himself being a Northerner), and especially the Jesuits, would give no help to priests arriving from the seminaries; he also said that in passage through London he had to spend several days in an inn without facilities for Mass, and at a
50 solemn season. Dismayed by this news, some priests, due to leave the College, could hardly summon up the courage to set out on their journey home to England. But when on arrival they found no one at all but ours [i.e. Jesuits] ready to afford help, advice, money for their needs, clothing even and shelter, they wondered
55 what manner of man this priest could be who made this report, as they themselves told me later, with no small amusement. As for his complaint that hospitality on that occasion was not readily forthcoming in London, there is here not the slightest cause for wonder. So closely are the houses of Catholics watched, that it is
60 out of the question to introduce anyone into them without greatest precaution and considerable thought. It so happened, in fact, that I and this priest came into London on the very same day. When I came to an inn at which to halt and before I had visited a single Catholic, I went out to pay a call on a man for business and out of
65 friendship. I could not take this priest with me, for I did not myself yet know whether a Catholic family would be found willing to shelter me for that night. Hardly had I gone twelve paces on leaving this priest than I came upon a good friend, a Catholic. I recommended this priest to him, and straightway he
70 went after him, but lost track of him, somehow missing him in the maze of streets. However, after a few days, he was entertained, with the greatest kindness, in the house of a Catholic of standing. But now we have in him too, one who is disposed to be most friendly to us, and one who is utterly opposed to that faction
75 which you have in Rome. . . .

> The Wisbech Stirs, 1595–8, ed. P. Renold (Catholic Record Society, vol LI, 1958), p 169

Questions

a   What is the common name of the Society of Jesus?

b   What light do these extracts shed on the difficulties and dangers facing English Catholics, particularly priests returning from Europe? Were all the difficulties 'external'?

* c   Outline the parts played by Edmund Campion and Henry Garnet in the sustaining of Catholicism in Elizabethan England. What was their fate?

d   It has been suggested that Catholic revival in England was hampered by the tendency of priests to attach themselves to gentry householders in preference to missionary work. Do these extracts support or challenge this suggestion?

e   By their own statements expressed in this extract, what were the highest priorities of returning Catholic priests?

III 'The Chief Riches of the Inhabitants' – Society and the Economy

Introduction

Our evidence of Elizabethan society, trade and the industrial and agricultural economy tells us so much and so little. On the one hand we have the dazzling pageant of life revealed in literature, chronicles and contemporary descriptions, but much of this evidence is subjective, anecdotal and patchy. On the other hand modern economic historians have laboured to produce a statistical base for evidence of industrial production, of population sizes and movements, of prices, land values and the standard of living.

All this evidence has been pressed into service in historical debate. The classic debate, originating with Tawney and Trevor Roper, concerns the 'rise of the gentry', and has been summed up in Lawrence Stone's study of social change and revolution. Perhaps the force of the debate has diminished since its arguments have been less used in discussion of the origins of the Civil War, and since precise and detailed studies of particular places or families have taken the place of the broad canvas on which the controversy began. Yet the debate itself stood as a model for subsequent reassessments of the past. The student should consider the form of the debate: thesis, antithesis and a dissolution of the debate into detail: and ask what the strengths and weaknesses of this model are. Is it conducive to the most vigorous and rigorous possible historical enquiry, or does it become an exercise in posturing and self-justification?

What the Civil War has been to the history of Elizabethan society, the Industrial Revolution has been to the study of Elizabethan industry. Rather than being studied for its own sake, pre-eighteenth-century industry has been scrutinised for the evidence it can furnish of continuity and lack of development, but these extracts will provide a little material for discussion of these questions: what was the scale of industrial activity in Tudor times? Is there evidence for changes in technique, organisation or application which would make an industrial 'revolution' possible? How far was the wealth-making potential of industry appreciated by contemporaries in general and law-makers in particular? Likewise with trade: how well comprehended were the prospects for England as a centre for trade and finance, or as a mother of colonies?

No introduction could do justice to Elizabethan culture and society. It has been described in terms of a renaissance and fine flowering but inevitably for most people daily life had more preoccupations than joys, and society was impregnated with inequalities and tensions; between age and youth, male and female, town (and court) and country, lower and higher 'degree'; and the student will be able to add to the list.

1 Frobisher's gold

(a) 1577: Captain Frobisher, in a ship of our Queen's, of the burden of 200 tons, came into Kingroad [where the Avon joins the Severn] from Cathay [in fact from North America], who brought certain ore from thence, which was esteemed to be very
5   rich and full of gold; it was heavy, and so hard that it would strike fire like flint; some of it was tried in our castle, and the rest sent to London, where it was esteemed not worth the charges in refining. They brought likewise a man called Callicho, and a woman called Ignorth: they were savage people [Eskimos] and fed only upon
10 raw flesh. The 9th of October he rowed in a little boat made of skin in the water at the Back [the quay], where he killed two ducks with a dart, and when he had done carried his boat through the Marsh upon his back; the like he did at the weir and other places where many beheld him. He would hit a duck a good
15 distance off and not miss. They died here within a month.
        Adams's Chronicle of Bristol (1623, Arrowsmith, 1910), p 115

(b) 1576 . . . . Those monied men being persuaded [of the existence of the North West Passage], sent Martin Frobisher with three pinnaces to discover this strait, who setting from Harwich on the 18th of June, entered the 9th August into a bay or strait
20 under the latitude of 63 degrees, where he found men with black hair, broad faces, flat noses, swarthy coloured, apparelled in sea calves' skins, the women painted about the eyes and balls of the cheek with a blue colour like the Ancient Britons. But for that all was so frozen with ice in the month of August, that he could not
25 hold on his voyage, he returned, and arrived in England the 24th of September, having lost five sailors whom the barbarians had intercepted. Nevertheless, the two years next following, he sailed to the same coasts to finish his enterprise; but being encountered everywhere with heaps of ice like mountains, he was kept from
30 entering any farther into the bay. Being therefore tossed up and down with the foul weather, snows and inconstant winds, he gathered a great quantity of stones, which he thought to be

minerals, and so turned homewards; from which stones, when
there could be drawn neither gold nor silver, nor any other metal,
35 we have seen them cast forth to mend the highways. . . .

> William Camden, *The History of the Most Renowned and
> Victorious Princess Elizabeth* (1630), Book 2, p 79

(c) Notes framed by Mr. Richard Hakluyt of the Middle Temple
Esquire, given to certain gentlemen that went with Mr. Frobisher
in his North-west discovery, for their direction. . . .
Now admit that we might not be suffered by the savages to
40 enjoy any whole country or any more than the scope of a city, yet
if we might enjoy traffic, and be assured of the same, we might be
much enriched, our navy might be increased, and a place of safety
might there be found, if change of religion or civil wars should
happen in this realm, which are things of great benefit. But if we
45 may enjoy any large territory of apt soil, we might so use the
matter, as we should not depend upon Spain for oils, sacks,
raisins, oranges, lemons, Spanish skins etc. So we should not
exhaust our treasure, and so exceedingly enrich our doubtful
friends, as we do, but should purchase the commodities that we
50 want for half the treasure that now we do, and should by our own
industries and the benefits of the soil there cheaply purchase oils,
wines, salt, fruits, pitch, tar, flax, hemp, masts, boards, fish, gold,
silver, copper, tallow, hides and many commodities: besides if
there be no flats to make salt on, if you have plenty of wood you
55 may make it in sufficient quantity for common uses at home
there.

> Richard Hakluyt, *Principal Navigations, Voyages, Traffics and
> Discoveries of the English Nation*, vol V (Everyman), pp 165,
> 168

Questions

a What do extracts *a* and *b* suggest about popular perceptions of
voyages of exploration in Elizabeth's reign? Are there any
differences of emphasis between the two extracts?

b What are Hakluyt's arguments for establishing colonies? What
light do his arguments shed on English anxieties and fears at
the time?

c To what extent are Hakluyt's expectations of the extent of
colonisation limited?

★ d Compare the exploration and colonisation efforts made in
Elizabeth's reign with those of the periods before and after.

2 Industry and Agriculture

(a) Mendip miners

[A document of Mary's or Elizabeth's reign]

The old ancient custom of the occupation in and upon the Queen's Majesty's Forest of Mendip within her Grace's County of Somerset being one of the four staples of England which has been
5 exercised and continued through the said forest from the time whereof man has no memory as hereafter does particularly appear.

First of all, if any man whatsoever he be that does intend to venture his life and to be a workman of the occupation, he must first of all require licence of the Lord of the soil where he does
10 purpose to work, or in his absence his officer called the head Reeve or Bailiff, whereupon the Lord nor his officers cannot by the old custom of the occupation deny him that does so ask licence. . . .

Item: that when any workman has landed any ore he may carry
15 it to washing and blowing to what 'myndry' [smelting house] he seems best for his profit and commodity so that he does pay the tenth of that in lead or ore to the Lord of the soil where it was digged etc.

Item: that if any Lord or Lords of the 'myndrys' or his officers
20 have or hereafter do once give licence to build or set up any hearth or hearths, house or houses to wash and blow their ore in, the tenant once so having licence may keep it, sell it or give it for ever to whom it shall please him without any let or contradiction so that he do use himself justly and truly and paying the 'lot lead',
25 the which is the tenth of the flight and profit of that hearth. . . .

Item: and if any man of that occupation do pick or steal any lead or lead ore to the value of thirteen pence, the Lord or his officer may arrest and seize upon all his lead and lead ore, hearth and house, gruff and grooves [workings] and to keep it at a forfeit to
30 his own use and behove, and shall take the person that so offended and bring him where his house and ore is, his work and tools and all instruments belonging to that occupation, and then put him in his house or working place and set fire in all together about him and banish him from that occupation for ever before the face of all
35 the miners. . . .

Item: and if that said person so ever offend any more in that occupation by picking or stealing then he shall be committed to the Queen's jail for the occupation has no more to do with him. . . .

40 Item: The Lord or Lords of every soil upon Mendip ought to keep a court two times every year and to call the miners together and to choose twelve of the honestest men and to swear them for the redress of all misdemeanours as concerning that occupation. . . .

Item: and if there be any man by this doubtful and dangerous
45 occupation do take his death and is slain by falling of the earth
upon him, by drowning, by stifling with fire or otherwise as in
times past many have been so murdered, the coroner nor no
officers of the Queen's Majesty have not to do with the body nor
with his or their goods but the miners of that occupation shall
50 fetch up that dead body out of the earth at their own proper costs
and charges and also to bury him in Christian burial although he
do take his death forty fathoms deep under the earth, as here
before many a man so has been lost. . . .

> *Mendip Mining Laws and Forest Bounds*, ed. J. W. Gough
> (Somerset Record Society, vol XLV, 1931), pp 6–8

(b) *Iron versus timber*

An Act that timber shall not be felled to make [char]coals for the
55 making of iron.

For the avoiding of destruction and wasting of timber, be it
enacted . . . that no persons hereafter shall convert or employ, or
cause to be converted or employed to [char]coal or other fuel for
the making of iron, any timber tree or timber trees of oak, beech
60 or ash or of any part thereof, of the breadth of one foot square at
the stub, and growing within fourteen miles of the sea or any part
of the rivers of Thames, Severn, Wye, Humber, Dee, Tyne, Tees,
Trent or any other river, creek or stream by which carriage is
commonly used by boat or other vessel to any part of the sea. . . .
65 Provided always that this Act shall not extend to the County of
Sussex nor to the Weald of Kent, nor to any of the Parishes of
Charlwood, Newdigate and Leigh in the Weald of the County of
Surrey. . . .

> 1 Elizabeth c.15 (1559), *Statutes of the Realm*, vol IV, Part I,
> p 377

(c) *Coal and metals*

Of coal mines we have such plenty in the north and western parts
70 of our island as may suffice for all the realm of England, and so
must they do hereafter indeed, if wood be not better cherished
than it is at present. And to say the truth, notwithstanding that
very many of them are carried into other countries of the main
[i.e. of the continent], yet their greatest trade begins now to grow
75 from the forge into the kitchen and hall, as may appear already in
most cities and towns that lie about the coast, where they have
little of other fuel except it be turf and hassock [a kind of turf]. I
marvel not a little that there is no trade of these [coals] into Sussex
and Southamptonshire [Hampshire], for want whereof the smiths
80 do work their iron with charcoal – I think that far carriage be the
only cause, which is but a slender excuse to enforce us to carry
them into the main from hence. . . .

Tin and lead . . . , are very plentiful with us, the one in Cornwall, Devonshire, and elsewhere in the North, the other in

85 Derbyshire, Weardale and sundry places of this island, whereby my countrymen do reap no small commodity, but especially our pewterers, who in time past employed the use of pewter only upon dishes, pots and a few other trifles for service here at home, whereas now they are grown so exquisite cunning that they can in

90 manner imitate by infusion any form or fashion of cup, dish, salt, bowl or goblet which is made by goldsmith's craft though they be never so curious, exquisite and artificially forged. . . .

Iron is found in many places, as in Sussex, Kent, Weardale, Mendip, Walsall, as also in Shropshire, but chiefly in the woods

95 between Buildwas and Wenlock [in Shropshire] . . . and elsewhere in Wales. Of which miners diverse do bring forth so fine and good stuff as any that comes from beyond the sea, beside the infinite gains to the owners, if we would so accept it or bestow a little more cost in the refining of it. . . . Nevertheless, it was

100 better cheap with us when strangers [foreigners] only brought it hither, for it is our quality, when we get any commodity to use it with extremity towards our own nation, after we have once found the means to shut out foreigners from the bringing in of the like. It breeds in like manner great expense and waste of woods. . . .

William Harrison, *The Description of England* (1577), ed. Georges Edelen (Cornell U.P., 1968), pp 363–9

(d) Wool

105 [Sheep are] more cherished in England than stands well with the commodity of the commons or prosperity of diverse towns, whereof some are wholly converted to their feeding; yet such a profitable sweetness is found in their fleece, such necessity in their flesh, and so great a benefit in the manuring of barren soil

110 with their dung and piss that their superfluous numbers are the better borne withal. And there is never an husbandman (for now I speak not of our great sheepmasters, of whom some one man has twenty thousand) but has more or less of this cattle feeding on his fallows and short grounds, which yield the finer fleece. . . .

Ibid., p 130

(e) The fat of the land

115 The soil is fruitful, and abounds with cattle, which inclines the inhabitants rather to feeding than ploughing, so that near a third part of the land is left uncultivated for grazing. The climate is most temperate at all times, and the air never heavy; consequently maladies are scarcer, and less physic is used there than anywhere

120 else. There are but few rivers: though the soil is productive, it bears no wine, but that want is supplied from abroad by the best

kinds, as of Orleans, Gascon, Rhenish and Spanish. The general
drink is beer, which is prepared from barley, and is exceedingly
well tasted, but strong and which soon fuddles. There are many
125 hills without one tree, or any spring, which produce a very short
and tender grass, and supply plenty of food to sheep; upon these
wander numerous flocks, extremely white, and whether from the
temperature of the air, or goodness of the earth, bearing softer and
finer fleeces than those of any other country: this is the true
130 Golden Fleece, in which consist the chief riches of the inhabitants,
great sums of money being brought into the island by merchants,
chiefly for that article of trade. . . . Glasshouses are here in plenty.
> Paul Hentzner, *Travels in England during the Reign of Queen
> Elizabeth*, trans. Horace Walpole (London 1797), pp 62–3

Questions

a   What privileges and what responsibilities of the miners are
    revealed in extract *a*? What insights does the extract give into
    working practices?
b   Does the evidence in this section (extracts *a–e*) suggest that
    industrial activity was marked by continuity and stasis or by
    change and expansion?
c   From the evidence given in extracts *b* and *c*, identify the main
    locations of the iron industry in Tudor times. Which location
    was favoured by statute?
* d   Explain what Harrison means by 'far carriage' (line 80). Was
    he right to cite this as the only reason why iron ore was not
    smelted with coal?
e   What evidence is there in extracts *b* and *c* of change and
    development in the techniques or volume of industrial
    production?
f   What hints are made about the connection between pro-
    tectionism and monopolies? On what grounds does Harrison
    criticise the English preference for native products?
g   Identify in geological and geographical terms the 'hills without
    one tree . . . (extract *e*, line 125).
h   How does Harrison, in extract *d*, categorise the 'positive' and
    'negative' economic effects of sheep-farming? Can you explain
    Hentzner's less critical account of English sheep-farming in
    extract *e*?

3   Stuart Financial Expedients Forshadowed

(a) 9 November 1596
A letter to the Lord Archbishop of York and the rest of the
Council there. Whereas the town of Kingston-upon-Hull did set
forth a ship in warlike manner to join with her Majesty's navy the

5   last summer, the charge whereof . . . does amount to £1400
     towards the which they have received as yet of the City of York
     only the sum of £600, and therefore they have been humble
     suitors to us to have some aid of the towns of Halifax, Wakefield
     and Leeds . . . or out of other parts of the shire and other clothing
10   towns within the West Riding, to bear part of this burden . . . .
     We directed our letters accordingly, and on the other side those of
     the aforesaid towns do allege diverse reasons whereby they desire
     to be exempted to contribute with the port of Hull. . . .

     7 December 1596
15   A letter to the Deputy Lieutenants of the County of Dorset.
     Whereas we have earnestly required you by diverse letters in the
     behalf of the town of Weymouth and Melcombe Regis to assist
     them with a small contribution out of the County of Dorset
     amounting but to £160 towards the charge of almost £400
20   wherewith they are charged for the setting forth of a ship in the
     late service to Cadiz . . . we have cause to conceive some dislike
     of this your neglect of care in a matter tending to the service of
     her Majesty and the general good of the realm . . . .

     27 February 1597
25   . . . We have written unto you heretofore so often for the
     contribution out of that country toward the charge of the ship set
     forth in the late voyage to Cadiz from the port of Weymouth as
     we cannot but think a great contempt by you committed in the
     little regard that seems to be had of our letters, and her Majesty's
30   service hindered by the ill example of such slackness, whereby the
     owners of that ship and mariners that remain unpaid as also the
     inhabitants of that and other parts may hereafter be made the less
     willing to employ themselves upon like occasion another time,
     which slackness deserves the more blame because the sum to be
35   collected is no more than £160 throughout the whole county, and
     the same not only remains unsatisfied but our directions also are
     without answer from you. . . .
     [The Privy Council conducted similar correspondences with
     other counties.]
     Acts of the Privy Council 1596–7, pp 304, 353, 527–8

40   (b) Knights be not born, neither is any man a knight by succession,
     no, not the King or Prince . . . for as 'equites Romani' [Roman
     Knights] were chosen 'ex censu', that is, according to their
     substance and riches, so be knights in England most commonly
     according to their yearly revenues or abundance of riches
45   wherewith to maintain their estates. Yet all that had 'equestrem
     censum' [been assessed as a knight] were not chosen to be knights,
     and no more be all made knights in England that may spend a
     knight's lands, but they only whom the Prince will honour.

Sometimes diverse, ancient gentlemen, burgesses and lawyers are
50 called to knighthood by the Prince and nevertheless refuse to take
that state upon them, for which they are of custom punished, by a
fine that redounds to his coffers and, to say truth, is oftentimes
more profitable to him than otherwise their service should be if
they did yield to knighthood. . . .

William Harrison, *The Description of England*, op cit,
pp 101–2

Questions

a What light does extract *a* shed on procurement of ships and
supplies?
b From the evidence of extract *a*, where does the initiative to
extend ship money to inland towns originate?
c Why was the call to knighthood not an unmixed blessing
(extract *b*)?
★ d Did Charles I exploit ship money and the bestowal of honours
in the same way that Elizabeth did?

4 Social pecking order

(a) *Society mobile*

[Merchants] often change estate with gentlemen, as gentlemen do
with them, by a mutual conversion of the one into the other . . .
[their] number is so increased in these our days that their only
maintenance is the cause of the exceeding prices of foreign wares,
5   which otherwise, when every nation was permitted to bring in her
own commodities [i.e. in her own ships], were far better cheap
and more plentifully to be had . . . . I do not deny but that the
navy of the land is in part maintained by their traffic, and so are
the high prices of wares kept up. Now they have gotten the only
10 sale of things, upon pretence of better furtherance of the
commonwealth, into their own hands; whereas in times past,
when the strange bottoms [foreign ships] were suffered to come
in, we had sugar at fourpence the pound that now, at the writing
of this treatise [1577] is well worth half-a-crown, raisins or
15 currants for a penny that now are holden at sixpence, and
sometimes at eightpence and tenpence the pound, nutmegs at
twopence halfpenny the ounce, ginger at a penny an ounce,
prunes at halfpenny farthing [¾ penny], great raisins three pound for
a penny, cinnamon at fourpence the ounce, cloves at twopence
20 and pepper at twelve pence and sixteen pence the pound. . . .

Yeomen are those which by our law are called 'legales homines',
freemen born English, and many dispense of their own free land
in yearly revenue to the sum of forty shillings sterling [£2], or £6
as money goes in our times. . . . This sort of people have a certain

25 pre-eminence and more estimation than labourers and the common
sort of artificers, and these commonly live wealthily, keep good
houses and travail [work hard] to get riches. They are also for the
most part farmers to gentlemen . . . or at the leastwise artificers;
and with grazing, frequenting of markets and keeping of servants
30 (not idle servants as the gentlemen do, but such as get both their
own and part of their masters' living) do come to great wealth,
insomuch that many of them are able and do buy the lands of
unthrifty gentlemen, and often, setting their sons to the schools,
to the universities, and to the Inns of the Court, or otherwise
35 leaving them sufficient lands whereupon they may live without
labour, do make them by those means to become gentlemen. . . .
William Harrison, *The Description of England*, op cit,
pp 115–17

(b) *Society immobile*

Sumptuary laws against rich apparel.
Elizabeth R.
Whereas the Queen's Majesty, for avoiding of the great incon-
40 venience that has grown and daily does increase within this her realm
by the inordinate excess in apparel, has, in her princely wisdom and
care for the reformation thereof, by sundry former proclamations
straitly [i.e. strictly] charged and commanded those in authority
under her to see her laws provided in that behalf duly executed.
45 Whereof notwithstanding . . . no reformation at all has followed.
Her Majesty, finding by experience that by clemency . . . this
increasing evil has not been cured, has thought fit to seek to
remedy the same by correction and severity. . . . In regard of the
present difficulties of this time, wherein the decay and lack of
50 hospitality appears in the better sort in all countries [i.e. districts],
principally occasioned by the immeasurable charges and expenses
which they are put to in superfluous apparelling their wives,
children and families; the confusion also of degrees in all places
being great where the meanest are as richly apparelled as their
55 betters, and the price that such inferior persons take in their
garments driving many, for their maintenance, to robbing and
stealing by the highway. . . .
For men's apparel:
Her Majesty does straitly charge and command that none shall
60 wear in his apparel,
Cloth of Gold or silver tissued ⎫
Silk of colour purple ⎭ under the degree of an Earl
Cloth of gold or silver
Tinselled satin ⎫
65 Silk or cloth mixed or embroidered with ⎬ under the degree
pale gold or silver ⎪ of a Baron
Woollen cloth made out of the realm ⎭

For women's apparel:

70
Cloth of gold or silver tissued
Silk of colour purple
} under the degree of a Countess

Cloth of gold
Cloth of silver
Tinselled satin
Satin branched with silver or gold
75 Satin striped with silver or gold
Taffetas branched with silver or gold
Taffetas with gold or silver grounds
Tinselled taffetas tufted or plain
Tinselled cypresses
80 Cypresses flourished with silver or gold
Gold or silver camlets
Networks wrought with silver or gold
Tabinets branched or wrought with silver or
gold or any other silk or cloth mixed or
85 embroidered with pearl, gold or silver etc.
} under the degree of a Baroness

The Egerton Papers, ed. J. Payne Collier (Camden Society, 1840), pp 247–52

Questions

a What benefit of a large merchant fleet does Harrison allow?
★ b How profound is Harrison's analysis of inflation?
★ c Outline the 1601 parliamentary crisis over monopolies, which Harrison criticises in extract *a*.
★ d How close is Harrison's analysis of social mobility to any of the twentieth-century models of rise and fall between classes in Tudor England?
e Which of the prohibitions in extract *b* appears to be protectionist in intention?
f From the evidence of extract *b* what model of society does Elizabeth's government favour?

5 Houses

The greatest part of our building in the cities and good towns of England consists only of timber, for as yet few of the houses of the commonalty (except here and there in the West Country towns) are made of stone, although they may (in my opinion) in
5 diverse other places be built so good cheap of the one as of the other . . .

This also has been common in England, contrary to the custom of all other nations and yet to be seen (for example) in most streets in London, that many of our greatest houses have outwardly been
10 very simple and plain to sight, which inwardly have been able to

receive a Duke with his whole train and lodge them at their ease. Hereby moreover it is come to pass that the fronts of our streets have not been so uniform, and orderly built as those of foreign cities, where (to say truth) the utterside [outside] of their mansions
15 and dwellings have oft more cost bestowed upon them than all the rest of the house, which are often very simple and uneasy within, as experience does confirm. Of old time, our country houses instead of glass did use much lattice, and that made either of wicker, or fine rifts [strips] of oak in checkerwise. . . . But as horn
20 in windows is now quite laid down in every place, so our lattices are also grown into less use, because glass is come to be so plentiful and within a very little so good cheap, if not better than the other.

There are old men yet dwelling in the village where I remain,
25 which have noted these things to be marvellously altered in England, within their sound remembrance. One is the multitude of chimneys lately erected. . . . The second is the great amendment of lodging, for, said they, our fathers and we ourselves have lain full oft upon straw pallets covered only with a sheet under
30 coverlets made of bagswain or hop harlots (I use their own terms) and a good round log under their heads instead of a bolster. . . . The third thing they tell of, is the exchange of treen [wooden] platters into pewter, and wood spoons into silver or tin.

William Harrison, *The Description of England*, op cit, pp 195–7

Questions

a What indications does Harrison give of recent and future improvements in house-building?
★ b Prof. W. G. Hoskins has written of a 'great rebuilding' in the 1590s. What evidence have we of this?
c What does Harrison think are the priorities of the English compared to foreigners?
d Are Harrison's observations supported by the evidence of the extracts on industry and agriculture (Section 2)?
e Does the extract suggest rising or falling standards of living among common people?

6 O Tempora! O Mores!

The argument of tragedies is wrath, cruelty, incest, injury, murder, either violent by sword or voluntary by poison: the persons, gods, goddesses, furies, fiends, kings, queens and mighty men. The groundwork of comedies is love, cozenage, flattery,
5 bawdry, sly conveyance of whoredom: the persons, cooks, queens, knaves, bawds, parasites, courtesans, lecherous old men, amorous

young men. The best play you can pick out is but a mixture of good and evil; how can it be then the schoolmistress of life? The beholding of troubles and miserable slaughters that are in tragedies
10 drive us to immoderate sorrow, heaviness, womanish weeping and mourning, whereby we become lovers of dumps and lamentation, both enemies to fortitude. Comedies so tickle our senses with a pleasant vein that they make us lovers of laughter and pleasure without any mean, both foes to temperance. What
15 schooling is this? Sometime you shall see nothing but the adventures of an amorous knight, passing from country to country for the love of his lady, encountering many a terrible monster made of brown paper, and at his return is so wonderfully changed, that he cannot be known but by some posy in his tablet,
20 or by a broken ring, or a handkercher [sic], or a piece of cockle shell. What learn you by that? . . . In my opinion, the discipline we get by plays is like to the justice that a certain schoolmaster taught in Persia, which taught his scholars to lie and not to lie, to deceive and not to deceive, with a distinction how they might do
25 it to their friends and how to their enemies; to their friends for exercise, to their foes in earnest. Wherein many of his scholars become so skilful by practice, by custom so bold, that their dearest friends paid more for their learning than their enemies. . . .

Stephen Gosson, *Plays Confuted in five actions* (1582), in J. Dover Wilson, *Life in Shakespeare's England*, pp 158–9

Questions

★ a What do Elizabethan tastes in literature and drama seem to have been from the evidence of this extract?
   b From what standpoint does this critique seem to have been made?
★ c Identify some Elizabethan playwrights or storytellers whom Gosson might have criticised.

7 The Way We Live

(A medicine for the falling sickness taught by Mrs. Stacey)

'Take an old toad and slay it, then split him and take out all his inwards, saving his liver. . . . Wash it very clean, and lay it on a tile stone in an oven after the bread is drawn, and dry it and make
5 a powder of it and mix therewith a small quantity of cinnamon, and give the party in ale or beer as much as will fill a hazel nutshell full at one time: it must be taken after the party has fallen of his disease and they must fast after it four or five hours. . . .

The claws of the toad must be cut off. . . .'

10   (Housekeeping list for Christmas week, 1594)
        Wheaten bread 16 dozen [40 oz] loaves
        Brown bread 28 dozen loaves
        Beer 8 hogsheads [each 52½ gallons]
        Beef 50 stone
15   Mutton 6 carcases, 1 joint
        Pork 27 joints 8 pigs
        Blackbirds 6 dozen
        Larks 8 dozen
        Rabbits 50; also geese, hens and wild game
20   Flour 9 pottles [each half a gallon]
        Candles 36 lbs
        Butter (fresh) 15 lbs
        Butter (salt) 35 lbs
        [The domestic labour of three maids and seven men]:
25   Of the three maids one is to serve for cook, one for tending of
     poultry, making butter and cheese and necessaries, the third for a
     chambermaid or otherwise at your pleasure; of the seven men
     servants, one to bake and brew, one to tend your ground and
     make your provisions of beef and mutton and to serve as caterer.
30   Two to attend on yourself, one of them to serve in the buttery,
     and in his absence one of the maids or the brewer. One to keep
     the horse. A warrener to serve as a caterer when your other
     servant shall be abroad for making other provisions, lastly a
     footboy.
        Quarterly Review, vol 215, 1911, pp 131–5. 'An Elizabethan
        Gentlewoman: the Journal of (Grace) Lady Mildmay, born
        c. 1552'

Questions

   a   To what extent had the influence of American and Far Eastern
       foods and spices entered Lady Mildmay's household?
   b   To what degree were Lady Mildmay's servants specialists?
 ★ c   'Folk remedies' are commonly represented as the medicine of
       the poor. What explanations can you offer for Lady Mildmay's
       interest in Mrs Stacey's remedy?

IV   'Poor, aged and impotent people' – Poverty and Social Provision

Introduction

The causes of poverty in Elizabethan England have been analysed many times. The headings in John Pound's study of poverty and vagrancy could be rearranged as follows: there is no doubt that war, a rising population, harvest failures and price inflation (arising partly from the destabilisation of bullion prices after the first arrival of gold and silver from America) bore heavily upon many. More arguable are the effects of fluctuations in the clothing industry, of the dissolution of the monasteries and of enclosure. Historians earlier this century drew pessimistic conclusions about the impoverishment of the common people in late Elizabethan England. R. H. Tawney sought to fit such conclusions into a dialectic socialist interpretation of Tudor and Stuart history. We should beware of overoptimistic revisions, but Joan Thirsk, for example, has shown how complex, and often positive, the economic results of enclosure were.

The phenomenon of poverty is easier to record. All kinds of documents reveal a preoccupation in Elizabethan times with scarcity and 'dearth' (dearness), vagrancy, urban 'unemployment' (our word) and rural hunger. Motives for wishing to take action or see action taken ranged from the strictly moral, through a desire to protect the economic state of the nation, to plain fear of uprising. It is no longer possible to share the opinion of many in Tudor times, especially in the north, that the dissolution of the monasteries marked the end of charitable response to poverty on a large scale. W. K. Jordan suggested that charitable bequests increased in the late sixteenth century, but Lawrence Stone challenges that Jordan made no allowance for inflation. Nevertheless Paul Slack, in Christopher Haigh's volume on the reign of Elizabeth, concludes that 'Puritans' were probably more generous and positively active in poor relief than our modern preconceptions might allow.

Responses to poverty ranged from private, through 'corporate' to statutory. However varied these responses were in their motives, methods and effectiveness, the Elizabethan vagrancy and poor laws stand as an increasingly systematic approach to the problems, providing for parish poor rates, punishments for vagabonds and various devices for relief, including licensed begging, censuses of the poor, apprenticeship and the workhouse; many of the Law's remedies were themselves adapted from the examples of individual towns.

1   Causes of Poverty: Inequality and Profiteering

(a) 'What it is rightly to consider of the poor'

Concerning this point, there be six propositions of special importance to be considered of.

1. The proceeding causes of so many poor in all countries.
2. That God might have made our estate like unto theirs.
5   3. That we should do to them as we would be done unto.
4. Why we all ought to help to relieve them.
5. Those places of scripture tending to compassion.
6. How their present want may be relieved.

To begin with the first proposition touching the proceeding cause
10 of many poor in all countries; though some impute the same to the dearth of grain, and the occasion thereof to unseasonable weather, especially in harvest time, by tempestuous winds which shake out the corn when it would have been shorn, yet we must search further from whence those came. . . .

15   For the former of these last causes, all winds and ill-weather proceed directly from the justice of God. . . .

The due premeditation whereof will urge us to consider of these particular sins which procure God's justice to punish us with penury.

20   1. Partly proceeding from the poor themselves.
2. Yet more especially from the poor-makers.

The proceeding sins from the poor themselves, whereby they provoke the Lord to pinch them, are these six especially.

1. First, their misspending of former times, in idleness, when
25   they might have wrought. [worked]
2. Secondly, their wilful wasting of their goods when they had them in bibbing [drinking] and belly-cheer.
3. Thirdly, their impatient bearing of their present want, complaining, often without cause.
30   4. Fourthly, their daily repining at others' prosperity, to have so much, and they so little.
5. Fifthly, their banning and cursing, when they are not served as themselves desire.
6. Sixthly, their seldom repairing to their parish churches, to
35   hear and learn their duties better, all which must be amended, if they would have their wants supplied.

The proceeding sins from the poor-makers, whereby they provoke God's justice to plague us with this present penury, in all places, are many and grievous, especially ten, which may be
40 termed the breeders of the poor:
1. All excessive proud persons in apparel.
2. The unmeasurable wasters of meat and drink.
3. The importable [unbearable] oppression of many landlords.
4. The unconscionable extortion of all usurers.
45 5. The insatiable covetousness of corn-mongers.
6. The wilful wrangling in Law matters.
7. The immoderate abuse of gaming in all countries.
8. The discharging of servants and apprentices.
9. The general abuse of all God's benefits.
50 10. The want of execution of good Laws and Statutes.

> *Provision for the Poor now in Penury* . . . , Henry Arth (1597), in R. H. Tawney and E. Power, *Tudor Economic Documents*, vol III, pp 450–2

(b) A Monopolist

[Original in Latin.]

1574: The jurors for our Lady Queen represent that William Smythe, late of Acton in the County of Middlesex aforesaid,
labourer, on the 8th day of October, in the 15th year of the reign
55 of our Lady Elizabeth by the Grace of God of England (etc.), at Acton aforesaid, bought from Randolph Cokerell, Rector of Acton aforesaid, eight cartloads of wheat, in sheaves, then being of the value of sixteen pounds, seven cartloads of rye in sheaves, then being of the value of fourteen pounds, and ten cartloads of
60 oats in sheaves, then being of the value of ten pounds, with the intention of selling the grain from there, being of the value of forty pounds of legal English money, and the same grain he engrossed [i.e. hoarded and monopolised to make a profit] against the substance of the statute published and provided for this kind of
65 case.

> *Middlesex Guildhall, General Sessions of the Peace Rolls*, 183, in R. H. Tawney and E. Power, op cit, vol I, p 155

Questions

a What social and moral lessons does Arth wish to impart to the poor in particular?

b Some of the sins which he identifies were responsible for poverty in what we might call a 'theological' sense. Which of the sins of the 'poor-makers' were *directly* responsible for poverty in Elizabethan England?

c How far does extract *a* support, and how far undermine, the proposition that puritan doctrine tended to emphasise the responsibility of the poor for their own plight?

d Which of Arth's sins was William Smythe guilty of?

e Why was it culpable of William Smythe to store grain, and laudable of the London authorities (Section 6b) to do so?

2 Causes of Poverty: Enclosure

(a) A poetic attack on enclosure

I know where there is a thief and long has been
Which spoileth every place where he resorts.
He steals away both subjects from the Queen
And men from his own country of all sorts.
5   Houses by three and seven and ten he razeth,
To make the common glebe his private land:
Our country cities cruel he defaceth,
The grass grows green where 'little Troy' did stand,
The forlorn father hanging down his head,
10 His outcast company drawn up and down,
The pining labourer doth beg his bread,
The ploughswain seeks his dinner from the town.
     O Prince, the wrong is Thine, for understand,
     Many such robberies will undo thy Land.

*   *   *

15 Sheep have ate up our meadows and our downs,
Our corn, our wood, whole villages and towns.
Yea, they have ate up many wealthy men,
Besides widows and orphan children;
Besides our statutes and our iron laws
20 Which they have swallowed down into their maws.
     Till now I thought the proverb did but jest
     Which said a black sheep was a biting beast.

*   *   *

When the great forest's dwelling was so wide,
And careless wood grew fast by the fireside:
25 Then dogs did wont the shepherd's fields to keep;
Now we want foxes to consume our sheep.
     'Chrestoleros', III, 22, IV, 20 and VI, 8, from *The Poems
     . . . of the Rev. Thomas Bastard*, in R. H. Tawney and E. Power,
     op cit, vol III, pp 80–1

(b) Reasons for resisting enclosure

Observations [by Robert Cecil?] on the statutes of the 39th year of
Elizabeth, C.1. and 2. [These Acts were against the destruction of
buildings and to promote the restoration of arable land in
30   preference to pasture.]
        Objections and answers or advantages upon them.
        If some do object strictness and impossibility, and others that
the law is too easy and will not work the effect we seek, advantage
may be taken that it shows the good temper of the law, and it will
35   ill beseem the gravity of the House if that which perhaps if it were
violently penned would get passage by the heat and animosity of
one side, being moderately penned, and not according to humour
but reason, shall find the fewer friends. That the laws for building
which are in force, and those for tillage which were in force till the
40   last Parliament, did no great good. To this it may be said the
laws were too many and too strictly penned to be kept.
        General reasons of state for both bills, both that of buildings
and that of tillage.
        The great decay of people. The engrossing [monopolising] wealth
45   into few hands. Setting people to work in husbandry, whereby
idleness, drunkenness and vice are avoided. Swarms of poor, loose
and wandering people bred by these decays, miserable to
themselves, dangerous to the State. Subjecting the realm to the
discretion of foreign states either to help us with corn in times of
50   dearth or to hinder us by embargoes on our cloths, if we stand too
much upon that commodity. Danger of famine. Some remedy
expected in the country . . . .
        Calendar of the MSS of the Marquis of Salisbury, vol XIV,
        Addenda, p 27

Questions

a   What varieties of rural activity and land use have been
       displaced by sheep runs according to the poems?
b   How much store does the poet set by statutes against enclosures
       (extract *a*)?
★   c   If you had been a contemporary of the poet, what arguments
       might you have used in defence of enclosure?
d   On what two grounds does the author of extract *b* argue for
       anti-enclosure legislation that is not too 'violently' or 'strictly'
       penned (lines 36 and 41)?
e   What wider issues does the author of extract *b* raise about the
       trend towards sheep-farming in place of arable farming?

3 Causes of Poverty: Bad Harvests and 'Dearth'

(a) Variable efforts by the Council of Bristol

1585: This year, by the good provision and love of Mr. Thomas
Aldworth of Bristol, merchant and Mr. James Cullimore of
London haberdasher, five ships laden with wheat, rye, malt and
barley from King's Lynn and Boston, to the value of £2,600 was
5   [sic] brought to this city, at the charges of the said Mr. Aldworth
and Mr. Cullimore, which did relieve Wales and Severn to the
great comfort of all the country thereabouts. For corn and all sorts
of grain was very scarce here: wheat was sold for 7 shillings a
bushel and the poor commons were ready to rise for lack of
10 money to buy it; for work grew scant with them by reason of the
imbarment [embargo] in Spain, but they were quickly pacified by
the good industry of the mayor and council, who caused Pensford
bakers to come every day in the week to the city with bread to
furnish them.
15   Mr. Mayor likewise hearing of a barque in Hungroad [near the
mouth of the River Avon], wherein was good store of butter
bound for France, went down himself and seized on it. The sailors
at first resisted him and abused him in words; notwithstanding he
unloaded the butter and brought 140 kilderkins into the Back
20 Hall, and sold it to the commons in the market for 2½ pence per
pound; and imprisoned the mariners for disobedience.
Also for the provision of this city here came in great store of
corn from Danzig, which made the prices to abate and did much
good . . . .
25   1595: This year all manner of corn began to be very dear, and
Mr. John Whitson, merchant, bought, in the month of November
by order from the Mayor and aldermen 3000 quarters of Danzig
rye of Mr. Thomas Offely of London, merchant, at 28 shillings
the quarter, to be delivered to Mr. Whitson here free of all charges
30 before the last of May next ensuing; but the said Mayor . . .
disliked the bargain, alleging it to be too dear, in regard it was so
long before the rye would come; whereupon the said Mayor and
aldermen would pay but one half of the charges and expenses that
Mr. Whitson had laid out . . . so that Mr. Whitson was to stand
35 to one half of the charges and to one half of the bargain himself.
But so it fell out that when the said rye was arrived in Bristol it
was well worth 44 shillings a quarter and more. And then the said
Mayor and aldermen entreated to have the whole bargain, and
would pay Mr. Whitson £50 for his charges and running the
40 adventure of the bargain; whereunto after some persuasions he
(being of a good nature) consented. And within 20 days after, this
rye was all sold at 5 shillings a bushel, much under the rate of the
market; many pecks and half bushels were given away among the

poor of this city. And, in conclusion there was gained upon this
45 bargain £774. . . .

1596: This year was such a dearth of all sorts of grain throughout
our land, that if the Lord of His mercy had not supplied our want
with rye from Danzig, most miserable had our case been as well
with rich as poor. To relieve the poor every alderman and
50 worshipful man, and every burgess of this city that was of any
worth, were appointed every day to find with victual at his table
so many poor people that wanted [i.e. lacked] work, whereby the
poor of our city were all relieved, and kept from starving or
rising.
55 [N.B. 8 bushels = 1 quarter]

Adams's Chronicle of Bristol, (1623, Arrowsmith, 1910),
pp 119–20, 149, 153

(b) Injustice to a grain merchant?

[3rd December, 1597] . . . Martin Frederico, a merchant of Venice,
has procuration from the Signory [governing Body] of Venice to
follow a cause concerning certain corn that was sold out of the 'St.
Agatha Marisina', which ship was the last year driven into
60 Portsmouth, and in regard of the great scarcity at that time within
the realm a good quantity thereof after appraisement was sold for
the use of the inhabitants of Portsmouth, Southampton and the
country thereabout. Forasmuch as the said Frederico does complain
that the corn was undervalued, sold at low prices and that there is
65 a great part wanting and of other abuses in the commissioners
appointed to sell the same. . . .

Acts of the Privy Council, vol XXVII, 1597–8, p 167

Questions

a What evidence is there in extract *a* that the shortage of food in
1585 was not universal?
b What light does the 1595 episode shed on the attitude of the
council of Bristol?
c Compare this attitude to that of the council of 1585.
d What factor in addition to the high price of grain is cited as a
cause of distress in the 1596 entry of extract *a*?
e What were the motives of the councils in seeking to relieve the
poor?
f What potential for injustice existed in the practice of buying up
rural supplies or ships' cargoes?
★ g From the evidence of your studies, and from reading this
chapter and Chapter V, how accurate is W. G. Hoskins'
description of 1595 to 1598 as a 'Great Famine'?
★ h Discuss the relationship of cause and effect between bad
harvests, enclosure, population growth and inflation.

4 Causes of Poverty: War

An injured veteran

[Wednesday 31 December 1561]: Edward Abbott being examined this day of the order of his begging says that it was in manner as follows:—

5   I desire your mastership to be good and friendly to a poor man that has been hurt and maimed in the Queen's affairs; maimed in my arm as your mastership may well perceive.

Q. Alack, good fellow – that is great pity! How came it to pass?

A. I was hurt with a piece of ordnance if it may please your mastership.

10   Q. Where did you serve when that you were hurt?

A. I served in one of the Queen's galleys called 'Speedwell' and was hurt being in the narrow seas.

Q. How long is it since you were hurt?

A. I was hurt at Whitsuntide was twelvemonth.

15   Q. Who was then Captain of that galley?

A. Captain Holden was Captain of that galley.

Q. In what conflict were you hurt?

A. I was hurt between Portsmouth and the Isle of Wight being matched and coupled with one of the French King's ships.

Records of the City of Norwich, eds Hudson and Tingey, vol II (1910), p 180, in R. H. Tawney and E. Power, op cit, vol II, pp 312–13

Question

★   *a*   In what ways might English people be reduced to poverty by the effects of war in Elizabethan times?

5 Responses to Poverty: Private

(a) The great fire of Nantwich

The Lords of the Council to William Chadderton, Lord Bishop of Chester. Whereas, by misadventure of fire [which] happened within the town of Nantwich in the County of Chester upon the tenth day of December last, there was burnt and consumed . . . to

5   the number of 800 houses [more likely about 150], with the most part of the goods and household stuff of the inhabitants to a very great value, whereby a great number of the said inhabitants, being men of good wealth, are, with their wives, children and families, utterly spoiled and undone; and the town become desolate, which

10   of late was not only of good wealth and trade by reason of [its] situation; but also of good importance for the service of her Majesty and the realm (being a thorough-fare, lying convenient

for the receipt of soldiers, carriages, and munition to be sent unto the realm of Ireland).

15 The Queen's Majesty therefore, of her gracious disposition, having herself [given] towards the relief of the said inhabitants a good value [she had contributed £1000], hoping that her loving subjects will also have consideration of the lamentable estate of these poor afflicted inhabitants, as they would desire relief of
20 other[s], upon the like visitation from God's hands:

To that end it has pleased her Majesty to command us most earnestly, in her name, to recommend the same unto your Lordship, and to require you, not only by your own good example in contributing in some reasonable manner, but by
25 dealing effectually with your clergy to yield their devotion the more largely, to further so charitable and necessary a purpose. . . .

From Westminster, the 9th of March 1584.

James Hall, *History of the Town and Parish of Nantwich* (1883), p 106

(b) The queen stirs up the north

[Queen Elizabeth to the Archbishop of York, the President of the Council of the North and others: 13 September, 1592.]

30 Forasmuch as we are credibly informed that many colleges, hospitals and almshouses, and other rooms and places within this our realm which have been founded and ordained, some of them by us and our progenitors and some of them by diverse other godly and well disposed persons, for the charitable relief of the
35 poor, aged and impotent people, are of late years greatly decayed and impoverished, and that the possessions and revenues thereof, . . . are unlawfully and most uncharitably converted to the private lucre and gain of some few greedy and covetous persons, contrary to the godly intent and meaning of the founders and givers
40 thereof, and to the great offence of Almighty God: know ye that we being moved with a most godly zeal to have all such poor, aged and impotent people, and specially soldiers and mariners, and other our [*sic*] good subjects which have been or may be hurt or maimed in the wars for maintenance of God's religion, and for
45 the defence of us and their native country, to be godly and charitably provided for, relieved and maintained . . . . [We] have therefore chosen you to be our Commissioners, and do by these presents assign and appoint, and give full power and authority to you, or any three or more of you, to do and execute for and
50 touching the premises by search and view of evidences, examination of witnesses upon oath to be produced or called before you . . . by your precepts or commandment, inquisition by verdict of twelve or more lawful men, and by any other good and lawful ways and means whatsoever, as to your wisdom and discretion
55 shall be thought meet, all things and matters which are

contained and specified in certain articles annexed to this our
Commission. . . . Provided nevertheless that this our commission
or anything therein contained shall not in any wise extend to any
College, Hall or Houses of Learning within the Universities of
60 Cambridge or Oxford, or either of them, for any matter
concerning the order or government of any such Colleges, Halls
or Houses there, but only to enquire what lands, tenements, rents
or profits have been given to the said Colleges, Halls or House for
the maintenance or relief of alms people, or mending of bridges or
65 highways, or for exhibition or maintenance of poor scholars. In
witness whereof we have caused these our letters of commission
to be sealed with our great seal. Witness ourself at Kew, the 13th
day of September in the five and thirtieth year of our reign.

> *The Egerton Papers*, ed. J. Payne Collier (Camden Society,
> 1840), pp 161–3

(c) A charitable bequest

John Haydon of Cadhay Esquire gave unto this City certain
70 monies for the relief to be given to the poor yearly for ever at the
feasts of Easter and Christmas, that is to say 40 shillings in money
to the parishioners of Kenn to be bestowed by them yearly in
bread among the poor people of that parish for ever. And also to
the ten cells [almshouses] of Exeter 46 shillings 8 pence yearly
75 among them to be divided. That is to say to every of them 4
shillings 8 pence by the year which is 13 pence [should be 14
pence] a piece quarterly. As is witnessed by his Deed made the 6th
day of March, in the 30th year of the Queen's Majesty's Reign
1588 and is for the discharging, releasing and performance of the
80 last will and testament of David Hentsley, parson of Kenn late
deceased.

> 'John Hooker's Description of Exeter', *Devon and Somerset
> Record Society* (1919 and 1947), p 725

Questions

a By what route did the request for help reach the clergy of
  Chester diocese from townspeople at Nantwich?
b In what ways do Elizabeth and the Privy Council encourage
  private contributions to charity?
c What interest did the Government have in the rebuilding of
  Nantwich?
d What contemporary trends were tending to detract from the
  value or effective use of charitable bequests?
★ e In what ways did the sources, direction and emphasis of
  private charity and bequests shift between the early sixteenth
  century and Elizabeth's reign?

6 Responses to Poverty: Corporate

(a) Licence to beg

Letter of Commendation. To all Mayors, Justices, Sheriffs, Bailiffs
and other her [*sic*] Majesty's officers to whom these presents shall
come, Robert Chaffe, Mayor of the City of Exeter, greeting.
Forasmuch as the bearer hereof, George Sampford of this City,
5   tooker [tucker] and Ede, his wife, being without work, are
desirous to travel to some convenient place where they may have
work for their better relief, and also having with them one child:
these are therefore to pray you, to whom these presents shall
come, quietly to permit and suffer these bearers hereof to seek for
10 work for their better relief without any of your let, molestation or
trouble. In witness whereof to these presents I, the said Mayor,
have set my hand and seal. Given the 8th day of June, in the 19th
year of the reign of our Sovereign Lady Elizabeth etc. [1577].
[This document finally came to rest in Chester.]

> R. H. Morris, *Chester in the Plantagenet and Tudor Reigns*,
> p 358, in R. H. Tawney and E. Power, op cit, vol II, p 334

(b) London's grain store under scrutiny

15 [The Privy Council questions the Lord Mayor of London]
Q. First, what grain have you of the provision of the city or
    brought of all sorts and what quantity of every sort and in
    what garners and where is the same bestowed?
A. We say for answer that in the Bridgehouse there is now in
20   wheat 1212 quarters, [a quarter is 28lb] in rye 231 quarters, in
    barley 521 quarters, in oats 10 quarters, in malt 60 quarters, in
    toto – 2034 quarters.
    In the white bakers' hands in wheat and meal in their houses
    2174 quarters.
25   In the brown bakers' hands in mestlin [maslin: rye and wheat
    mixed]: 251 quarters.
    In the brewers' hands in malt and drink corn 3519 quarters and
    in wheat 148 quarters. . . .
Q. What several prices have you paid for the said corn, particularly
30   in every place and severally of every sort and in what shires
    within this realm and from whence out of this realm is the
    same bought?
A. We say the particular price of all sorts of grain and where they
    were bought do at large appear in the Bridgehouse book, in
35   the white bakers' book, in the brown bakers' book and in the
    brewers' book, which books are ready to be shown.
      The provision of the cooks of the most part has been bought
    in the meal market at uncertain price and also the provisions
    [of the?] bakers in the common ovens since Michaelmas last

40 was bought in the meal market at uncertain price out of the realm, the price being so high and the time so pressing we could not make provision. . . .

Q. That the Mayor do declare what extensions they have hereafter to amend this error in lack of provision of breadcorn.

45 A. We say that the city has been chiefly furnished with all kinds of grain for provision of the same from the shires lying westwards from the City and aptly conveyed to the City as well by land as by the river of Thames, as also from Kent, Sussex, Dorsetshire, Hampshire, Suffolk and Norfolk, and not out of
50 any foreign part but upon a sudden and mere extremity: and for the better furnishing of the City hereafter, having your honours' favour and licence to make provision in convenient shires within the realm, we have determined to have continually in the store houses and garners of this city 4000 quarters of
55 wheat and rye, being by two parts more than heretofore [we?] have been accustomed to furnish, and stay the meal markets within the City at reasonable price, as we have done since midsummer last and so presently do continue.

N. S. B. Gras, *Evolution of the English Corn Market*, pp 450–4, in R. H. Tawney and E. Power, op cit, vol I, pp 156–8

Questions

a How far was the Mayor of Exeter complying with existing legislation in extract *a* (see Section 7)?

b In extract *b*, what are the Privy Council trying to reassure themselves of?

c What are the Lord Mayor and Corporation trying to plead in respect of their foresight, the prices they have paid and the places of origin of the grain they have bought?

7 Responses to Poverty: Statutary

(a) A. J. P.'s interpretation of the law

An Upright Man: of these ranging rabblement of rascals, some be serving-men, artificers, and labouring men traded up in husbandry. These, not minded to get their living with the sweat of their face, but casting off all pain, will wander after their wicked manner
5 through the most shires of this realm; as Somersetshire, Wiltshire, Berkshire, Oxfordshire, Hertfordshire, Middlesex, Essex, Suffolk, Norfolk, Sussex, Surrey and Kent, as the chief and best shires of relief. Yea, not without punishment by stocks, whippings and imprisonment, in most of these places abovesaid. Yet,
10 notwithstanding they have so good liking in their lewd, lecherous loiterings, that full quickly all their punishments are forgotten:

and repentance is never thought upon until they climb three trees
with a ladder. . . .

    . . . There came to my gate the last summer, Anno Domini
15   1566, a very miserable man, and much deformed, as burnt in the
face, blear-eyed and lame of one of his legs, that he went with a
crutch. I asked him where he was born, and where he dwelt last,
and showed him that thither he must repair and be relieved, and
not range about the country; and when he had drunk, I demanded
20   of him whether he had ever been despoiled of the upright man or
rogue.

    'Yes, that I have', quoth he . . . .

        Thomas Harman, *Caveat for Common Cursitors*, in A. V.
        Judges, *The Elizabethan Underworld* (1930), pp 68–70, 98

(b) 1563 Poor Law

    . . . If it shall chance for any parish to have in it more poor and
impotent folk, not able to labour, than the said parish is able to
25   relieve, that then in every such parish not standing in any city or
town corporate, the parson, vicar or curate of the said parish, and
two or three of the chief inhabitants of the same parish, and in
every city and town corporate, the mayor or chief officers of the
same city or town corporate, and the parson, vicar or curate of the
30   same parish . . . shall certify to the Justices of Peace of the county
where the same parish is, the number and names of the persons
with which they be surcharged, and upon such certificate, the said
Justices of the Peace . . . shall then grant unto such and as many of
the said poor folks as by their discretion they shall think good, a
35   sufficient licence . . . to go abroad to beg, get and receive the
charitable alms of the inhabitants of the Country out of the said
parishes, cities and towns so surcharged . . . .

    . . . All and every such poor folks as by any such licence are to
be licensed and authorised . . . to beg, get and gather the charitable
40   alms of good people, shall at all times when the same go abroad to
beg, wear openly upon him or them, both on the breast and the
back of his or their uppermost garment, some notable badge as
token. . . .

        5 Elizabeth c.3 (1563), *Statutes of the Realm*, vol IV, Part I,
        pp 413–14

(c) 1572 Act for punishment of vagabonds and relief of the poor

[Whipping vagabonds and sending them to their native parish was
45   first prescribed by an Act of 1531.]

    . . . All the parts of this realm of England and Wales be
presently with rogues, vagabonds and sturdy beggars exceedingly
pestered, by means whereof daily happen in the same realm

horrible murders, theft and other great outrage, to the high
50 displeasure of Almighty God, and the annoy[ance] of the Common
Weal. . . .

. . . All and every person and persons whatsoever they be,
being above the age of fourteen years, being hereafter set forth by
this Act of Parliament to be rogues, vagabonds as sturdy beggars
55 . . . shall upon their apprehension be brought before one of the
Justices of the Peace or Mayor or chief officer . . . to be presently
committed to the Common jail of the said county. . . .

. . . If such person or persons be duly convict[ed] of his or her
roguish or vagabond trade of life . . . then immediately he or she
60 shall be adjudged to be grievously whipped, and burnt through
the gristle of the right ear with a hot iron of the compass of an
inch about. . . .

And forasmuch as charity would that poor aged and impotent
persons should as necessarily be provided for, as the said rogues,
65 vagabonds and sturdy beggars repressed . . . the Justices of the
Peace, Sheriffs, Bailiffs and other officers . . . shall . . . make
diligent search and enquiry of all aged, poor, impotent and
decayed persons born within their said divisions and limits, or
which were dwelling within three years next before this present
70 parliament, which live or of necessity be compelled to live by
alms of the charity of the people . . . and shall upon that search
made . . . make a register book containing the names and surnames
of all such aged, decayed and impotent poor people. . . .

14 Elizabeth c.5 (1572), *Statutes of the Realm*, vol IV, Part I,
pp 590–3

(d) 1598 Poor Law

Be it enacted . . . that the churchwardens of every parish, and
75 four substantial householders . . . shall be called Overseers of the
Poor of the same parish, and they or the greater part of them shall
take order from time to time . . . for setting to work of the
children of all such whose parents shall not by the same persons be
thought able to keep and maintain their children, and also all such
80 persons married or unmarried as having no means to maintain
them, use no ordinary and daily trade of life to get their living by:
and also to raise weekly or otherwise (by taxation of every
inhabitant and every occupier of lands in the same parish in such
competent sum and sums of money as they shall think fit) a
85 convenient stock of flax, hemp, wool, thread, iron and other
necessary ware and stuff to set the poor on work, and also
competent sums of money for and towards the necessary relief of
the lame, impotent, old, blind and such other among them being
poor and not able to work. . . . And . . . it shall be lawful for the
90 said churchwardens and overseers, or the greater part of them, by
the assent of any two Justices of the Peace, to bind such children

as aforesaid to be apprentices, where they shall see convenient, till such man child shall come to the age of four and twenty years, and such woman child to the age of one and twenty years. . . .

> 39 Elizabeth c.3 (1598), *Statutes of the Realm*, vol IV, Part II, pp 896–7

(e) 1598 Act for Punishment of Vagabonds

95 . . . And be it enacted . . . that every person which is by this present Act declared to be a rogue, vagabond or sturdy beggar, which shall be, at any time after the said feast of Easter next coming, taken begging, vagrant, wandering or misordering themselves in any part of this realm or the dominion of Wales,
100 shall upon their apprehension . . . be stripped naked from the middle upwards and shall be openly whipped until his or her body be bloody and shall be forthwith sent from parish to parish by the officers of every the same the next straight way to the parish where he was born, if the same may be known by the party's
105 confession or otherwise; and if the same be not known, then to the parish where he or she last dwelt before the same punishment by the space of one year, there to put him or her self to labour as a true subject ought to do. . . .

> 39 Elizabeth c.4 (1598), *Statutes of the Realm*, vol IV, Part II, p 899

(f) 1601 Poor Law

[The bulk of the 1601 Act is a restatement and rationalisation of
110 the previous recent Acts.]

. . . to the intent that necessary places of habitation may more conveniently be provided for such poor, impotent people, be it ᵓnacted . . . that it shall and may be lawful for the said cᵤurchwardens and overseers, or the greater part of them, by the
115 leave of the Lord or Lords of the manor whereof any waste or common within their parish is as shall be parcel, and upon agreement with him or them made in writing . . . to erect, build or set up in fit and convenient places of habitation in such waste or common, at the general charges of the parish . . . to be taxed,
120 rated and gathered in manner before expressed, convenient houses of dwelling for the said impotent poor, and also to place inmates or more families than one in one cottage or house. . . .

> 43 Elizabeth c.2 (1601), *Statutes of the Realm*, vol IV, Part II, p 963

Questions

a How well does Harman (extract *a*) know the law (refer to extracts *b–f*)?

b Explain the expression 'climb three trees with a ladder' (lines 12–13).

c Citing specific terms, show in what direction the law's treatment of 'sturdy beggars' was moving during Elizabeth's reign.

d In what respects do the responsibilities and powers of the parishes grow during the same period?

★ *e* What were the social and economic implications of the 1598 Poor Law?

★ *f* By what name did the 'places of habitation' allowed for in the 1601 Poor Law become known?

★ *g* Was the distinction between vagabonds and 'impotent poor' really tenable? Compare Harman's specific cases with the general provisions of the Laws.

V 'Gathered together to resist by force' – Disorder and Rebellion

Introduction

Strong though the Tudor Monarchy appears to us, especially under the Henries and Elizabeth, two points must be remembered. Firstly, in the absence of a standing army or 'police', government depended heavily on consent, and some of these extracts show how sensitive Elizabeth's councillors were, not only to public disorder, but also to public opinion.

Secondly, every Tudor monarch had to face actual rebellion. The extracts in this chapter illustrate six features of disorder and rebellion. Foreign visitors and local records testify to an endemic tendency to violence in Tudor England (Sections 1 and 2). Economic grievances (Sections 2 and 3), religious principles (Section 4) and political in-fighting (Sections 4 and 5) provide three major ingredients of revolt. The Rebellion of the Northern Earls had strong religious and political roots, rural risings such as that attempted in Oxfordshire in 1596 had largely economic and social origins while the Earl of Essex's fiasco in 1601 was a more purely political event than that of 1569.

Each of these three features, economic, religious and political, needs close and exact historical scrutiny. Contemporary documents, modern statistical work and articles in historical journals can confirm or question assumptions made at the time, for example about the rate of enclosure in the south or the strength of Catholicism in the north. What mattered to rebels, noble or common, however, was their perception of their grievances, and what mattered to the authorities was their assessment of the seriousness of the danger.

Two other features should be considered. One is the tendency to disorder in the areas where the queen's writ scarcely ran, such as the Marches of Scotland (Section 6). Lastly, over many events, foreign influence cast a shadow (Section 7). Perhaps the potential influence of foreign ambassadors, spies, rulers and agents, Spanish and Papal, French and Scottish, was exaggerated both by the queen's ministers at home and by the foreign powers themselves. Burghley, Walsingham and other councillors never dropped their guard, however, against foreign stimulation of domestic unrest.

Some extracts display the last survivals of the medieval convention that rebels were loyal subjects protesting against bad advisers. As in earlier centuries this plea did not save failed rebels from the penalties of revolt against the throne.

1   A Tendency to Disorder

(a) A foreign visitor's view

[Jacob Rathgeb, The Duke of Württemburg's Secretary, visited London in 1592. Original in German.]

London is a large, excellent and mighty city of business and the most important in the whole kingdom; most of the inhabitants are employed in buying and selling merchandise and trading in almost every corner of the world. . . . The inhabitants are
5   magnificently apparelled and are extremely proud and overbearing; and because the greater part, especially the trades-people, seldom go into other countries, but always remain in their houses in the city attending to their business, they care little for foreigners, but scoff and laugh at them; and moreover one dare not oppose them,
10   else the street boys and apprentices collect together in immense crowds and strike to the right and left unmercifully without regard to person; and because they are the strongest, one is obliged to put up with the insult as well as the injury.

William Rye, *England as seen by foreigners in the Days of Elizabeth and James I* (1967), pp 7–8

(b) A libel by apprentices in London

After our most hearty commendation unto you good brethren and
15   apprentices, trusting in God that you are in good health as we were at the making hereof. The cause of our writing to you at this time is for to know whether you will put up this injury or no; for to see our brethren whipped and set on the pillory without a cause, which is a grief to us. Desiring you to send answer one way
20   or other, for if you will not put it up we do give consent to gather ourselves together upon [St.] Bartholomew's Day in the fields, some with daggers, some with staves, some with one weapon, some with another, such as may be least mistrusted, and to meet in the fields between Islington and London between three and four
25   of the clock in the afternoon against my Lord Mayor going to the wrestling, and there to be revenged of him; but if he go not to the wrestling, then to be revenged of him at his house where he dwells, and thus we end, committing you to God. AMEN.

Trevelyan Papers, Part II, ed. J. Payne Collier (Camden Society, 1863), p 101

(c) Rufflers and prigmen

A Ruffler goes with a weapon to seek service, saying he has been a
30 servitor in the wars and begs for his relief. But his chiefest trade is
to rob poor wayfaring men and market women.

A Prigman goes with a stick in his hand like an idle person. His
property is to steal clothes off the hedge, . . . or else filch poultry,
carrying them to the ale-house, which they call the boozing inn,
35 and there sit playing at cards and dice, till that is spent which they
have so filched.

> John Awdeley, *The Fraternity of Vagabonds* (1561), in A. V.
> Judges, *The Elizabethan Underworld* (1930), p 53

(d) Upright citizens come to blows

Forasmuch as Richard Gyfforde, butcher, and John Howell,
cordwainer, men of good reputation and who sometimes have
been Steward of the City, have very unseemly, disorderly and
40 indecently misdemeaned themselves not only in outrageous words
and terms but also in fighting and brawling that therefore the said
Richard Gyfforde shall abide in prison at the will and pleasure of
the Mayor and Twenty-four [i.e. Corporation] and pay the fine of
10 shillings, and the foresaid John Howell shall pay the fine of 3
45 shillings 4 pence.

28th December Anno 1° Elizabeth; 1558.

> John Hooker, *Description of the City of Exeter, Devon and
> Cornwall* (Record Society, 1919 and 1947), p 934

(e) Soldiers in Bristol

1565: This year came 700 soldiers to Bristol at the end of St.
James's Fair [July] which were bound for Ireland against the rebel
O'Neill; the wind being contrary they tarried here six weeks, in
50 which, some growing rude, three or four ruffians of them began a
brawl with the citizens at nine of the clock at night and though
many blows were given on each side, yet no man was killed by
reason the captains and magistrates came quickly thither upon
hearing of it, and soon appeased the matter. But afterwards
55 Captain Rendall, their general, making enquiry of the cause and
beginnings thereof, put the chief offenders of his men in prison in
irons, and two days after intended to execute martial law upon
them. A gibbet was erected in the midst of the High Street over
against the end of Mary le Port Street. All the soldiers were
60 commanded to come thither unarmed to see the execution; and
when the time and hour appointed for the execution [came], the
offenders being penitent, by much entreaty of the worshipful of
this [city], with other captains and gentlemen, the general forgave

them contrary to his purpose; but nevertheless put them from his
65 banner, he was so fiercely bent against them to maintain justice.
        Adams's Chronicle of Bristol (1623, Arrowsmith, 1910),
        pp 108–9

Questions

★ a How useful are foreign observations about England in Tudor
       times? What are the general strengths and weaknesses of such
       evidence? (Use extract *a* for some of your ideas.)
   b On what pretext did 'Rufflers', 'Prigmen' and the like wander
       the country with weapons?
   c What connections between war and disorder are suggested by
       extracts *c* and *e*?
   d According to extracts *d* and *e* what sort of force and penalties
       do Tudor town authorities seem to have had to help them
       overcome disorder?

2   A Magistrate's View of Vagabondage

Edward Hext, a Somerset J.P., to Lord Burghley, 25 September
1596.
Right honourable and my very good Lord.

      Having long observed the rapines and thefts committed within
5 this country where I serve, and finding they multiply daily to the
   utter impoverishing of the poor husbandman that bears the
   greatest burden of all services, and knowing your most honourable
   care of the preservation of the peace of this land, [I] do think it my
   bounden duty to present unto your honourable and grave
10 consideration these calendars enclosed of the prisoners executed
   and delivered this year past in this County of Somerset, wherein
   your Lordship may behold 183 most wicked and desperate persons
   to be enlarged. And of these very few come to any good, for none
   will receive them into service and in truth work they will not,
15 neither can they without most extreme pains, by reason their
   sinews are so benumbed and stiff through idleness as their limbs,
   being put to any hard labour, will grieve them above measure, so
   they will rather hazard their lives than work. . . . But my good
   Lord, these are not all the thieves and robbers that are abroad in
20 this County, for I know that in the experience of my service here,
   that the fifth person that commits a felony is not brought to this
   trial. . . . If they be [taken] and come into the hands of the simple
   man that has lost his goods and let them slip, because he will not
   be bound to give evidence at the assizes to his trouble and charge;
25 others are delivered to simple Constables and Tythingmen that
   sometimes wilfully, other times negligently, suffer them to escape;
   others are brought before some Justice that wants [i.e. lacks]
   experience to examine a cunning thief, or will not take the pains

that ought to be taken in sifting him upon every circumstance and presumption. . . . In default of justice many wicked thieves escape, for most commonly the simple countryman and woman, looking no farther than into the loss of their own goods are of opinion that they would not procure a man's death for all the goods in the world . . . and these that thus escape infect great numbers, emboldening them by their escapes. . . . I do not see how it is possible for the poor countryman to bear the burdens duly laid upon him . . . there be some that stick to say boldly, 'they must not starve; they will not starve'. And this year there assembled 80 in a company and took a whole cart load of cheese from one driving it to a fair and dispersed it amongst themselves, for which some of them have endured long imprisonment and fine by the judgment of the good Lord Chief Justice at our last Christmas Sessions, which may grow dangerous by the aid of such numbers as are abroad, especially in this time of dearth. . . . [They say] that the rich men have gotten all into their hands and will starve the poor. And I may justly say that the infinite numbers of the idle, wandering people and robbers of the land are the chiefest cause of the dearth, for though they labour not, and yet they spend doubly as much as the labourer who does, for they lie idly in the ale houses day and night eating and drinking excessively. And within these three months I took a thief that was executed this last assizes, that confessed unto me that he and two more lay in an alehouse three weeks, in which time they ate twenty fat sheep whereof they stole every night one; besides, they break many a poor man's plough by stealing an ox or two from him, and [he] not being able to buy more, leases a great part of his tillage that year. Others lease their sheep out of their folds, by which their grounds are not so fruitful as otherwise they would be. . . .

And when these lewd people are committed to jail, the poor country that is robbed by them are enforced there to feed them, which they grieve at. And this year there has been disbursed to the relief of the prisoners in the jail above £73, and yet they allowed but 6 pence a man weekly. . . . Of wandering soldiers there are more abroad than ever were, notwithstanding her Majesty's most gracious proclamation lately set forth for the suppressing of them, which has not done that good it would, if it had been used as it ought, for the Justices in every shire . . . ought to have . . . acquainted all inferior officers with it . . . but the proclamation being sent to the Sheriffs, they deliver them over to the Bailiffs to be proclaimed in the markets; there a few ignorant persons hear a thing read which they have little to do with and less regard, and the tenth justice knows not yet that ever there was any such proclamation. . . .

The inhabitants . . . made complaint at our last Easter Sessions . . . whereupon precepts were made to the Constables of the

Hundred, but few apprehended, for they have intelligence of all things intended against them, for there be of them that will be present at every assize, sessions and assembly of Justices and will so clothe themselves for that time as any should deem him to be
80 an honest husbandman. So as nothing is spoken, done or intended to be done but they know it. I know this to be true by the confession of some. . . .

At a late sessions, a tall man, a very sturdy and ancient traveller, was committed by a Justice and brought to the sessions and had
85 judgment to be whipped, he presently, at the bar, in the face and hearing of the whole bench, swore a great oath that if he were whipped it should be the dearest whipping to some that ever was; it struck such a fear in him that committed him as he prayed he might be deferred until the Assizes, where he was delivered
90 without whipping or any other harm and the Justice glad he had so pacified his wrath. . . . Knowing the danger that may grow by these wicked people to my dread and most dear Sovereign's most peaceable government, I will not leave it unadvertised, though I should hazard my life by it . . . from my poor house at Netherham
95 [Low Ham] in Somersetshire this 25th of September, your good Lordship's in all humbleness to be commanded, Edw. Hext.

Lansdowne MS No 81, Art 6, ff 161–2, in R. H. Tawney and E. Power, *Tudor Economic Documents*, vol II, pp 339–46

Questions

★ *a* In what ways did weaknesses in local justice – its mechanism, personnel and sentencing – make conviction of vagabonds difficult?
b By what tricks of their own did the vagabonds evade justice?
c What echoes do you find in lines 36–7 of the threats made in Norfolk and Oxfordshire (Section 3*a* and *d*)?
d How, according to Hext, do the activities of vagabonds directly worsen the incidence of shortage of food (lines 51–5)?
★ *e* What is the significance of the year of Hext's letter?

3 Economic Grievances

(This section is very closely connected to the material in Chapter IV.)

(a) A 'libel' in Norfolk

To the Mayor and justices of Norfolk

God save our Queen Elizabeth. For seven years the rich have fed on our flesh. Bribes make you justices blind and you are content to see us famished. What are these edicts and proclamations,

5   which are here and there scattered in the County concerning
     kidders, cornmongers and those devilish cormorants, but a
     scabbard without a sword, for neither are those murdering
     maltsters nor the bloody corn-buyers stayed. We thought to have
     pressed higher to our Lord Admiral, to entreat him to shut up the
10   gate of his gain awhile and content himself with that he has got.
     Sir William Paston, who might have been called Passion for his
     former pity, but now is Paston because he is become as hard as a
     stone. Woe to Hasselt [William Hassett?] who inhabits the
     seacoasts, that noble thief! . . . There are 60,000 craftsmen in
15   London and elsewhere, besides the poor country clown that can
     no longer bear, therefore their draught is in the cup of the Lord
     which they shall drink to the dregs and some barbarous and
     unmerciful soldier shall lay open your hedges, reap your fields,
     rifle your coffers and level your houses to the ground. Meantime
20   give licence to the rich to set open shop to sell poor men's skins.
     Necessity hath no law.
          Calendar of the MSS of the Marquis of Salisbury, vol XIII,
          Addenda, p 168

(b) The Oxfordshire rising discovered

A letter to the Lord Norris. Her Majesty being informed that
there are certain evil-disposed persons in that county of Oxfordshire
under your Lordship's Lieutenancy that purpose to gather
25   themselves together in some numbers under pretence to pull
down enclosures and that they to execute their further malicious·
purposes have an intent to seize upon the armour and horses of Sir
Henry Lee, Knight and other gentlemen. For the speedy preventing
of their lewd attempts, which otherwise may grow to further
30   mischief, we have thought good to require you, being Her
Majesty's Lieutenant of that county, to call unto you some Justices
of the Peace of whom you shall think meet to make choice . . . to
take present order to apprehend the ringleaders of these seditious
persons, and after you have strictly executed them to send the
35   principallest of them up hither with the executions taken of them
and to commit such of the rest as you shall apprehend and think
meet to be committed. December 12, 1596.
          Acts of the Privy Council, vol XXVI, 1596–7

(c) The rebels' plans

[Bartholomew Steer, carpenter, declared that]
     . . . after their rising, they would go to Mr. Powers and knock
40   at the gate, and keep him fast that opened the door and suddenly
thrust in: and . . . he with his falchion [a short, sickle-like sword]
would cut off their heads, and would not bestow a halter on them:
and then they would go to Mr. Barry's and despoil him and cut

off his head and his daughter's head and from thence they would
45 have gone to Rathbone's house, a Yeoman, and despoil him
likewise and from thence to Mr. George Whitton and despoil him
and thence to Sir Henry Lee and despoil him likewise and thence
to Sir William Spencer and despoil him and so to Mr. Frere and so
to my Lord Norris and so to London . . . and when the apprentices
50 hear that we be up, they will come and join with us . . . and he
was the rather inclined to think the same by reason of the late
intended insurrection in London, and that certain apprentices were
hanged.
    [This had occurred in 1595 although Steer possibly believed it
55 had happened more recently.]
        Public Records Office, SP.12/262/4: 'Examination of Roger
        Symonds', in *Past and Present*, No 107, May 1985

(d) The rebels are caught and questioned

Sir W. Spencer, Deputy Lieutenant to Lord Norris and Sir William
Knollys, Comptroller of the Household, Lords Lieutenant of
Oxfordshire.
    There was a rising planned at Enslow Hill of 200 or 300 seditious
60 people from various towns of that shire, with the desire of raising a
rebellion. They were to despoil the neighbouring gentlemen's
houses of their arms and horses and go towards London, where they
expected to be joined by the apprentices. I have bound the parties
concerned to appear at the assizes, but imprisoned Barth, Steer,
65 Carpenter and Roger Ibill, miller, who persuaded many into this
action. They have confessed little, but might do more if sent for and
sharply examined. I am daily apprehending others, but little can be
discovered till Steer or Ibill confess. They met when most of the
gentlemen of the Shire were to appear in the King's Bench, on a suit
70 between Mr. Browne and Mr. Hoare. They are chiefly young
unmarried men and not poor.
    Yarnton December 6, 1596
    Examinations before Sir Wm. Spencer:
    Roger Ibill of Hampton Gay, loader. Has heard divers poor
75 people say that there must be a rising soon, because of the high
price of corn. Barth. Steer told him that there would be such a
rising as had not been seen a great while. . . . November 23,
1596.
    Roger Symonds, carpenter, of Hampton Gay. Was told by
80 Steer that he need not work for his living this dear year, for there
would be a merry world shortly; he tried to persuade examinate
[*sic*] to join to pull corn out of rich men's houses and on his refusal
left him. . . . November 25, 1596
    Barth. Steer of Hampton Poyle, refuses to confess anything.
85 Nov. 26, 1596
    Roger Symonds further confessed that Steer, to encourage him,

told him 100 men were coming from Witney and others from other parts, who were all to meet on Enslow Heath. . . . December 5, 1596.

90   John Steer of Witney. Was told of the rising by his brother Bartholomew, who said there would be 200 or 300 people, not needy, from Woodstock, Bladon, Kirtlington etc., and they would go from one rich man's house to another and take horses, arms and victuals. . . . December 5, 1496.

95   The Council to the Lord Norris. We thank you for your pains in the examination of these seditious people. We desire you to send up Bartholomew Steer, Roger Ibill and James and Richard Bradshaw, the ringleaders in the conspiracy, by the High Sheriff and under guard, their hands pinioned and their legs bound under their horses
100   bellies and allow them no conference on the way; if needful, they should be watched at night, at the inns where they lodge. . . . December 14, 1596.

Sir W. Spencer and Sir Ant. Cope to Lord Norris . . . . Since leaving you at Rycote, we have examined Richard and James
105   Bradshaw, Edward Huffer, a very dangerous fellow and John Hoare, servant to Mr. Barry of Hampton Gay. . . . We have laboured night and day, but cannot get confessions to make up 20 of the number. Their practices will very hardly be discovered unless it be on the rack, which it is likely they will taste of when they come
110   before the Lords of the Council. . . . Barth. Steer has confessed all that Symonds charges him with. . . . Yarnton December 15, 1596. [Several rebels were condemned to death. Steer was not among them: it is supposed he died in prison.]
Calendar of State Papers Domestic 1596–7, pp 316–19

Questions

★   *a*   What circumstances sparked off rural unrest in 1596?
   b   Which classes of people does the writer of extract *a* claim were ready to rise against rich men?
   c   What were Steer's grievances against his intended victims?
   d   What expectations about London does Steer share with the Norfolk libel-writer (extracts *a* and *d*)?
   e   What light do these extracts shed on the level of vigilance of local officers and the methods of investigation used in the counties and by the Privy Council?

4   The Rebellion of the Northern Earls

(a) The origins of the rebellion

[Lord Hunsdon questions the Earl of Northumberland in 1572.]
   When did you first enter into this conspiracy?
   Answer: We first began to talk of these matters when the Duke [of Norfolk] went in displeasure from the Court to his home in

5   London and it was noted in Yorkshire that the Council was
wonderfully divided about the succession, that the Duke and other
noblemen had retired to their homes and that the realm would be
in a hurly-burly; so I sent to the Duke and assembled my friends
to know their inclinations. I and many gentlemen intended to join
10   the Duke, if the quarrel were for reformation of religion or
naming a successor, but not to hazard myself for the marriage.
This I fear made my enemies about her Majesty pick a quarrel
with me. On the Duke's repair to court, hearing that the reports
about naming a successor were untrue, I sought to forbear to stir.
15   Yet to keep in those gentlemen that had frankly taken my part, I
did not seem to mislike their earnestness in executing their
purpose, but put them off until at last I was driven to it
perforce. . . . The Earl of Westmorland was cold, and had never
attempted it, but through the earnest means of his wife. . . .
20   What was the intent and meaning of the rebellion?
Answer: Our first object in assembling was the reformation of
religion and preservation of the person of the Queen of Scots, as
next heir, failing issue of Her Majesty, which causes I believed
were greatly favoured by most of the noblemen of the Realm. I
25   hoped my Lord Leicester, and especially Lord Burghley, with his
singular judgement, had by this time been blessed with Godly
inspiration to discern cheese from chalk, the matters being so
evidently discoursed by learned divines, and they have sway about
the Prince, and would bring her Majesty to the truth: but being
30   deceived, I can only pray God to indue Her and them with His
grace to know and fear Him aright.
          Calendar of State Papers Domestic, Addenda, 1566–1579,
          pp 406–7

(b) The Northern Earls' declaration of rebellion

Thomas, Earl of Northumberland and Charles, Earl of
Westmorland, the Queen's most true and loyal subjects and to all
Her Highness's people, send greetings: – Whereas diverse new set
35   up nobles about the Queen's Majesty, have and do daily, not only
go about to overthrow and put down the ancient nobility of the
Realm, but also have misused the Queen's Majesty's own person,
and also have by the space of twelve years now past, set up and
maintained a new found religion and heresy, contrary to God's
40   word. For the amending and redressing whereof, diverse foreign
powers do purpose shortly to invade these realms, which will be
to our utter destruction, if we do not ourselves speedily forfend
the same. Wherefore we are now constrained at this time to go
about to amend and redress it ourselves, which if we should not
45   do and foreigners enter upon us we should be all made slave and
bondsmen to them. These are therefore to will and require you,
and every of you, being above the age of sixteen years and not

50 sixty, as your duty towards God doth bind you, for the setting forth of his true and Catholic religion; and as you tender the commonwealth of your country, to come and resort unto us with all speed, with all such armour and furniture as you or any of you have. This fail you not herein, as you will answer the contrary at your perils. God save the Queen.

British Museum Harleian MS. 6990, fol 44, in Sir C. Sharpe, *Memorials of the Rebellion of 1569* (1840) p 42

(c) The Earl of Northumberland explains himself after the event

Westmorland asked what the ground of the quarrel was to be.
55 They said Religion. He said 'No', for such quarrels were accounted rebellion in other countries and he would not blot his long stainless house. This happened as my cousin [Leonard Dacre] and I looked for, that we might excuse ourselves to the rest. We ever judged Westmorland was unwilling, but urged to the matter. We
60 then separated, my Lord returning home. Dacre I never saw since.

Then old Norton and Markenfeld came to me and said we were already in peril, through our often meetings, and must either enter the matter without the Earl [of Westmorland], or depart the realm; and it would be a great discredit to leave off a godly
65 enterprise that was looked for at our hands by the whole kingdom, many of whom would assist us. I bade them take time to consider; they were away 14 days, and then returned with other gentlemen of the Bishopric [of Durham], and some belonging to the Earl, who were forward in the matter. I objected that my Lord President
70 [of the Council of the North: the Earl of Sussex] suspected us, and would not let us escape; but I offered to write to the gentlemen of the county to know their mind. They answered coldly, and that stopped us awhile. I wished to consult the Earl of Derby, Queen of Scots and Spanish Ambassador. The first did not answer; the
75 other two thought it better not to stir.

Then our company was discouraged. I left my house on a false alarm and went to Lord Westmorland's on my own way to Alnwick. I found with him Markenfeld, all the Nortons, his two uncles, the two Tempests, John Swinburne and Sir John Nevill,
80 all ready to enter forthwith. We consulted; my Lord, his uncles, old Norton and Markenfeld were all earnest to proceed. Francis Norton, John Swinburne, myself and others thought it impossible, so we broke up and departed, every man to provide for himself. Lady Westmorland, hearing his, cried out, weeping bitterly, that
85 we and our country were shamed forever, and that we must seek holes to creep into. Some departed, and I wished to go . . . but when I found I could not get away, I agreed to rise with them.

Calendar of State Papers Domestic, Addenda, 1566–1579, pp 404–5

★   *a*   Outline the main events of 'this conspiracy'. What were the respective fates of the Duke of Norfolk and the Earls of Northumberland and Westmorland?

    b   What was 'the marriage' (line 11)?

    c   How far do the reasons given for the rebellion in extract *a* correspond to those proclaimed in extract *b*?

    d   Who were the 'new set up nobles' in extract *b* lines 34–35?

★   *e*   Besides their personal and religious grievances, the Northern Earls felt that Elizabeth was not using them 'correctly'. Compare their place in Elizabeth's system with what it had been in Mary's reign.

    f   Was the rebels' claim to wish to pre-empt foreign intervention an honest one?

5   The Earl of Essex's Rising

(a) *The Earl of Essex in London*

1601: The 8th February, the Earls of Essex, Rutland and Southampton, Sir Gilly Meyrick and others made an insurrection in London, hoping the citizens would have taken their part. Essex's purpose was to have taken the court and so to displace
5   some great men thereabouts that were his supposed enemies, intending no hurt to Her Majesty as he did protest and the world believe. About St. Paul's churchyard his passage was resisted where some of his company were slain, some hurt and himself shot through the hat. The Earls, seeing they could not prevail, fled
10   and were taken in the Earl of Essex's home. The Earl of Essex was committed to the Tower, and many others to several prisons, where the Earl was beheaded shortly after, without consent of Her Majesty, who would in no wise consent thereunto, but took it grievously and kept her bed and wore a mourning weed for his
15   death. He was buried both head and body. He took it upon his death, that he died a faithful true-hearted subject to his sovereign, though he deserved not for his sins committed against God to live any longer. And so he died Godly and patiently, praying unto the Lord with tears for mercy; and so ended his life, committing his
20   soul to God's hands. He was generally beloved throughout the whole land, both of rich and poor, who lamented his death more than ever did subjects for the death of any nobleman. The Earls of Rutland and Southampton were released from trouble, but many other of his confederates were executed.

      Adams's Chronicle of Bristol, op cit, p 158

(b) A proclamation against Essex

25 February 9th 1601: Proclamation that whereas the Earl of Essex,
with the Earls of Rutland and Southampton and other gentlemen,
their accomplices, being discovered in treason in Ireland with
Tyrone and also in England, did, on 8th February, imprison the
Lord Keeper, Lord Chief Justice and others of the Council, sent to
30 persuade him to disperse his disordered company, and lay open
his just complaints for redress, threatening to murder them if they
stirred, and traitorously issued into London, breaking into open
rebellion and pretending their lives were threatened and continued
in arms, killing diverse subjects, after proclamation of rebellion
35 read by the heralds; yet the said Earls and their accomplices being
now apprehended and in the Tower, and no citizens having helped
them, Her Majesty thanks them for their loyal persisting in their
duty, promises to be more careful for them than for herself, and
charges them to lay hold on the spreaders of slanderous rumours
40 against Government, as the rebels probably have instruments in
diverse places.

Calendar of State Papers Domestic, 1598–1601, p 545

Questions

a What was Essex's 'treason in Ireland' (line 27)? (See also
Chapter VII, Section 4b).
★ b Identify the 'great men thereabouts' (line 5).
c How do extracts a and b differ in emphasis and tone? Can you
account for those differences?

6 The Marches of Scotland

[Robert Carey, Lord Hunsdon's youngest son, was Warden of the
Middle March in 1598.]

The thieves hearing of my being settled there, continued still
their wonted course in spoiling the country, not caring much for
5 me, nor my authority. It was the beginning of summer when I
first entered into my office, but afore that summer was ended,
they grew somewhat more fearful. For the first care I took, was to
cleanse the country of our inbred fears, the thieves within my
March, for by them most mischief was done; for the Scotch riders
10 were always guided by them in all the spoils they made. God
blessed me so well in all my designs, as I never made a journey in
vain, but did that I went for.

Amongst other malefactors, there were two gentlemen thieves,
that robbed and took purses from other travellers in the highways
15 (a theft that was never heard of in those parts before). I got them
betrayed, took them and sent them to Newcastle jail and there
they were hanged.

I took not so few as sixteen or seventeen that summer and the winter following, of notorious offenders, that ended their days by
20   hanging or beheading.

    The Memoirs of Robert Carey, ed. F. H. Mares (1972), p 48

Questions

★ *a*   What particular difficulties existed in the Marches of Scotland for the enforcement of law and order during Elizabeth's reign?
   b   Who are the prime culprits in theft in the Middle March, according to Carey?
   c   How does Robert Carey's assessment of his own success as an enforcer of law differ from that of Edward Hext (Section 2)? How do you account for the difference?

7 Spies and Rumours

(a) *One Earl informs on another*

H[enry], Earl of Huntingdon to Mr. Secretary [Walsingham]. There is great expectation amongst the papists of Lancashire and Cheshire that the Earl of Derby will play as fond a part this year as the two Earls did last year. He has hitherto been loyal but has at
5   this time many wicked counsellors. There is one Browne, a conjurer, in his h[ouse] kept secretly. Uphalls, who was a pirate and had lately his pardon, could tell somewhat. He that carried Lord Morley [an exiled Catholic] over was also there within this se'n'night kept secretly. If you would send some faithful and wise
10 spy that would dissemble to come from D. Alva [the Duke of Alva] and dissemble popery y[ou] might understand all; for if all be true that is said, there is a very fond company in that house at present. Ashby, 24th August, 1570.

    Calendar of the MSS of the Marquis of Salisbury, vol XIII, Addenda, p 100

(b) *Seditious rumours*

May 1571: Thomas Longe [M.P.] was licensed to depart home
15 [from the Commons], but immediately after he was sent to Bridewell and on Whitsun eve the 2nd of May he sat upon the Pillory in Cheapside for his seditious words, viz., that the Queen should be dead, which he affirmed that, being at the Duke of Norfolk's house, one of the servants of the said Duke should so
20 say unto him and willed him to tell the same to others.

    John Hooker's Journal in the House of Commons 1571, Transactions of the Devonshire Association, vol XI, 1879, pp 483–4

(c) Mysterious spies

The 14th April [sometime before 1601] . . . did arrive from Calais
to Boulogne, two Englishmen about 50 and 30, both blond, who
being demanded, answered that they were come from Douai,
where they had been a year. These two, the 16th of the said
25   month, did hire a boat at Boulogne for 50 francs, which was an
extraordinary price, and in the night did embark. Upon the 17th
they landed beside Sandwich, sending back two letters, one of
which being directed to a man of this town of Boulogne is sent to
you; that thereby you may know the name of the house where
30   they lodge, the better to try them out. Whereas in that letter they
allege they did come from Velbye [Selby?] in Yorkshire by sea,
they dissemble and increase suspicion of them the more. Their
other letter is to Rouen, to one Mr. Morcovy at the sign of the
'Ape', requiring him to send their two young cousins (who be
35   now at Rouen) with speed to Boulogne to the house of one
Philemon Johnston, who shall show them to what place in
England to go, which is to one Read's house in Sandwich.
Therefore, if nothing can be learned of the same Read, at the
coming of the two young men, all must be discovered and 65 [the
40   Mayor of Boulogne] how soon they arrive here will hold them till
he advertise 60 [the Earl of Essex], for assuredly the two eldest
have been employed by 69 [England], or else 45 [the King of
Spain] hath sent them over now for evil offences. In the letter
written to the said Morcovy he is required not to put any clothes
45   on the young men but homely clothes lest they be marked in
England, which is also suspicious.
> *Calendar of the MSS of the Marquis of Salisbury*, vol XIV,
> Addenda, p 168

Questions

★ *a* Explain and comment on the position of the Earl of Derby
between Elizabeth's accession and his death in 1572. (The
Dictionary of National Biography will help you.)

   b Explain the reference to Douai in extract *c* (line 23).

   c Considering the three extracts, would you say that rumours
were a danger to Elizabethan authorities?

   d What insights do these extracts provide into Elizabethan
intelligence methods?

   e What level of danger from foreign interference is suggested by
these extracts?

★ *f* Use the evidence of the whole chapter to discuss the actual
threat posed to Elizabeth's throne and government by rebellions
and uprisings. How accurate was contemporary assessment of
the threat?

VI 'To have a free voice' – Parliament and the Constitution

Introduction

Elizabethan England had no written constitution, only an accretion of precedents, statutes and common law, and the commentaries of writers such as Sir Thomas Smith and William Lambarde. The scope and powers of, for instance, the Commons and of the J.P.s had matured over a couple of centuries and were open to considerable debate.

Debate continues in our time, too, especially on the relationship of Elizabeth to her parliaments. J. E. Neale represented the Elizabethan Commons as coming of age, in practice, privileges and confidence. To him the Queen's influence over parliament, through Lords, The Speaker and the Privy Councillors, was challenged by a homogenous body of Puritan gentry, foreshadowing the quarrels between James I and Charles I and their parliaments. This view is reinforced by narratives such as that of J. B. Black, which suggest that after the dangers of Mary Stuart and the Armada are past, 'a fin de siècle feeling, compounded of irritation and lassitude, hovered like a cloud over the political landscape'.

Against this orthodoxy, questions rather than alternative statements have arisen. G. R. Elton has broached some of them in Christopher Haigh's 'The Reign of Elizabeth I'. What were the interests of the gentry in Elizabeth's parliaments? Whom did they represent? Are they after all predominantly 'Puritan'? Is it under Elizabeth or earlier that the Commons 'matures', achieving parity with the Lords and having their privileges confirmed? To what extent did Elizabeth 'need' parliaments? Is confrontation or cooperation the keynote for most of the sessions of Elizabeth's Commons? What was the level of attendance of Elizabeth's bishops, lords and M.P.s? Do Cecil and the councillors ever represent parliament against Elizabeth rather than the other way round? How differently did the Commons and the Queen interpret freedom of speech in matters such as religion, Elizabeth's marriage and the succession?

As to 'local' government, in the shires, roles were certainly changing. J.P.s, judges of assize, sheriffs and Lords Lieutenant have each their function and a place in a hierarchy, but the reader may enquire in what directions burdens were shifting between these offices.

Spies, patronage and extra-parliamentary courts such as Star Chamber add their ingredients to the complex pattern of control, consultation and consent within which Elizabeth and her ministers worked.

1 Beginnings

(a) Sir Nicholas Throckmorton's advice to Queen Elizabeth on her accession to the throne, November 1558

. . . It may please you to call Mr. Cecil to exercise the room of Secretary about your person forthwith and no other until I may speak with your Highness . . . .

5 It shall be very requisite that your Highness do appoint some privy councillors to associate the old council and to sit with them. . . .

It may please you that all such as you shall admit into your presence may receive grace in your looks and words, but in any wise it may like your Highness to suspend your grants to all
10 persons with good words for a time.

For religion and religious proceedings I will not treat of at this time, and yet it may like to require the Lords to have a good eye that there be no innovations, no tumult or breach of order in these general words. . . .
15 Item, for the appointing a meet officer in the Tower of London for the time of your coronation, for the summoning your parliament, for creating noblemen and Knights of the Bath, for the manner and the persons of such as ought to be touched and called to reckoning for the usage of present prisoners, for the
20 nominating of meet officers to every place, for making you a better party in the Lord's house of parliament, for appointing a meet common house to your proceedings, for fit and serviceable gentlemen to be of your privy chamber, for the appointing a meet chancellor or keeper of the seal, and for nominating a meet
25 speaker in the common house and what matters shall be meet for this parliament, for nominating apt Commissioners to take a view of your whole revenue, debts, jewels, apparel, munition, navy, mints and sundry other things, it may please you to defer the resolution until I have played the fool in the discourse of them as I
30 have done in the premises. [Throckmorton proceeds to make long lists of names of persons recommended for office.]

Ed. J. E. Neale, *English Historical Review*, vol 65 (1950), pp 94–5

(b) The complexities of accession

In the meantime certain Commissioners were appointed for the
funeral of the deceased Queen [Mary], others for the coronation
that was to ensue. New commissioners were sent into Wales, and
35 the Marches of the North. Thomas, Earl of Sussex [was appointed
for Ireland, who] with a garrison of 320 horse and 860 foot, kept
that country either in obedience or awe. New commissions were
made to the Judges of the Law, to continue only until the end of
that term; but with exception, that they should not in the
40 meantime bestow any offices. All the Councillors of the State [i.e.
Privy Councillors] who had served Queen Mary, and favoured
the Religion then established, were again admitted to their proper
places [13 in number after the death of Sir Thomas Cheyney on 8th
December]; to these were adjoined William Parr, Marquis of
45 Northampton, Francis Russell, Earl of Bedford, Thomas Parr,
Edward Rogers, Ambrose Cave, Francis Knollys and William
Cecil, and, soon after, Nicholas Bacon, men of assured
understanding and truth, and well affected to the Protestant
Religion. All these the Queen ruled with such moderation, as she
50 was never obnoxious to any of them, and all devoted and addicted
to her.

New Justices and Sheriffs were appointed in every shire, and
writs went forth to summon a Parliament, against the time of
Coronation. Ambassadors were appointed to the Pope, to the
55 Emperor and other Princes of Germany, to the French King, to
the King of Spain, to the King of Denmark, and to the State of
Venice, to renew leagues, to remove all prejudice that might be
conceived, to perform unto them openly all ceremonies of State,
and secretly to search into their inclinations.

Sir John Hayward, *Annals of the first four years of the reign of
Queen Elizabeth*, ed. J. Bruce (Camden Society, 1840),
pp 11–12

Questions

a How far did Elizabeth follow Throckmorton's advice (compare
extracts *a* and *b*)?

b What was the point of the advice given in extract *a*, lines 7–10?

c What assumptions does Throckmorton make about the
monarch's influence over parliament?

d What problems of continuity had to be met on Elizabeth's
accession? How far did that continuity itself pose problems for
Elizabeth?

★ e How realistic is Hayward's assessment of Elizabeth's relationship
with her Privy Council?

2 The Virgin Queen

1560: She, out of her singular love to her country, was all this while so attentive to the public good, that in the meantime she almost quite put out of her mind the love of potent princes. For at the same time there sought to her for marriage, Charles, Archduke

5   of Austria, a younger son of the Emperor Ferdinand by mediation of the Count of Elphenstein: James, Earl of Arran, commended by the Protestants of Scotland, with purpose to unite by him the divided kingdoms of England and Scotland, which purpose was soon rejected, with commendation of the man: Eric, King of

10   Sweden by means of John, his brother, Duke of Finland, whom Gustavus their father had sent a little before into England for that purpose, having the more hope to speed, for that he was of the same religion with her . . . this great and singular love she acknowledged and commended; she answered, 'he should be

15   welcome, but she could not yet persuade herself to change her single life, most pleasing to her, for a married life . . .'

. . . But Charles of Austria hoped and expected that the House of Austria, which had been most fortunate by matching with the greatest princesses, should be greatened by the addition of England;

20   and also that by him the old religion should be, if not restored, then at the least wise tolerated. Neither did Queen Elizabeth at the first dash cut off his hope. For she made show openly, and protested before Elphenstein, and by letters to the Emperor, 'that amongst many most honourable matches propounded none was

25   more honourable than this with Charles of Austria . . . .'

. . . Adolphus also, Duke of Holstein, uncle to Frederick the second King of Denmark, being excited thereunto by the Dane to the end to break off the marriage with the Swede, came into England, being also rapt with hope of marriage by occasion of a

30   letter wherein Queen Elizabeth had wished that he were joined to the English in the same nearness as he had been in time past to the Spaniard, and most lovingly promised him kindness. To whom, after most honourable welcome, she bountifully gave the honour of the Garter, and a yearly pension, and by her singular kindness

35   bound the prince unto her . . . .

And at home also there were not lacking some which (as lovers use to do) feigned unto themselves vain dreams of marrying with her: namely Sir William Pickering, Knight, who had some nobility of birth, a mean estate, but some honour by his studies of good

40   arts, elegancy of life, and embassies in France and Germany: Henry, Earl of Arundel, a man of very ancient nobility, great wealth, but of declining age, and Robert Dudley, the Duke of Northumberland's younger son, who was restored in blood by Queen Mary, a man of a flourishing age and comely feature of

45   body and limbs, whose father and grandfather were not so much

hated of the people but he was as much favoured by Queen
Elizabeth . . . .

> William Camden, *The History of the Most Renowned and*
> *Victorious Princess Elizabeth* (1630), Book 1, pp 42–4

Questions

a   Why did Elizabeth encourage all her foreign suitors?

b   What evidence is there in lines 22–25 that Elizabeth played off
one suitor against another?

c   In lines 1–16, what reasons does Camden attribute to Elizabeth
for not hurrying into marriage?

★ d   Does Camden give sufficient reasons for Elizabeth's rejection
of her English suitors, or does your wider reading suggest
additional or different reasons?

3   Parliament

(a) The most high and absolute power of the realm of England is
in the Parliament. For as in war where the King himself in person,
the nobility, the rest of the gentility and the yeomanry is, there is
the force and power of England: so in peace and consultation
5   where the Prince is to give life, and the last and highest
commandment, the baronry for the nobility and lords, the knights,
esquires, gentlemen and commons for the lower part of the
common wealth, the bishops for the clergy to be present to
advertise, consult and show what is good and necessary for the
10   common wealth and to consult together, and upon mature
deliberations every bill or law being thrice read and disputed upon
in either House, . . . that is the Prince's and the whole people's deed:
whereupon justly no man can complain but must accommodate
himself to find it good and obey it . . . .
15   The Prince sends forth his rescripts or writs to every duke,
marquis, baron and every other lord temporal or spiritual who has
voice in the Parliament, to be at his great council of Parliament
such a day (the space from the date of the writ is commonly at the
least forty days): he sends also writs to the sheriffs of every shire
20   to admonish the whole shire to choose two knights of the
parliament in the name of the shire, to hear and reason, and to
give their advice and consent in the name of the shire, and to be
present at that day: likewise to every city and town which of
anciety [old] has been wont to find burgesses of the parliament,
25   so to make election that they might be present there at the first
day of the parliament. The knights of the shire to be chosen by all
the gentlemen and yeomen of the shire, present at the day assigned
for the election: the voice of the absent is counted for none.

Yeomen I call . . . who may dispend [dispose of] at the least forty
30 shillings [£2] of yearly rent of free land of his own. These meeting
at one day, the two who have the more of their voices be chosen
knights of the shire for that parliament: likewise by the plurality of
the voices of the citizens and burgesses be the burgesses elected.

Sir Thomas Smith, *De Republica Anglorum*, 1565, ed.
M. Dewar (1982), pp 78–9

Questions

a What was the qualification to participate in the election of
knights of the shire?

★ *b* Why does Smith not specify what the qualification was in the
boroughs?

★ *c* To what extent were Elizabeth's parliaments representative?

★ *d* Smith's analogy of war implies unity of purpose. In what
matters were Elizabeth and her parliaments at one, and in what
were they not?

(b) 4 April 1571: The Speaker's three petitions and the Lord Chancellor's and Queen's replies

. . . First, that every [one] of that House might have free access
for self and his men to the said Parliament and that none of them
might be molested, vexed or sorried. Secondly, that every man
might have free speech and without interruption or trouble to
5 speak his mind freely. Thirdly that if he coming in [with] any
message to her Highness should be mistaken and speak otherwise
than in his commission, that it might not be taken to the worst
nor any advantage to be had thereof.

To the first, the Lord Chancellor answers that every man there
10 came to the making and devising of good laws, and therefore
none there could or ought to make breach of any laws wherefore
if any man being in debt did procure himself to be of that House
to the end to defer his creditors it were unreasonable that any such
privilege should be granted. To the second that her Highness
15 thinks it not meet that any should have further liberty to speak or
talk in that House of any matter other than that which is there to
be proposed and that they should leave talking 'rhetoricè' and speak
'logicè'; to leave long tales which is rather an ostentation of wit
than to any effect and to deal with these things as there were to be
20 proposed: that going effectually to the matter they might dispatch
that which they were sent for and that they might the sooner
return home. To the third, the Queen understood well of [the
Speaker's] wisdom, gravity and learning and that she mistrusted
not of any such simplicity to be in him, but if it should so come to

25   pass she would bear therewith. This done the Queen arose wishing
they would be more quiet than they were at the last time.

> *John Hooker's Journal in the House of Commons, 1571*, in
> *Transactions of the Devonshire Association*, vol XI (1879),
> pp 474–5

(c) On Wednesday 30th May [Sir Simonds D'Ewes says 29th
May] the general pardon was read. These bills past, Sir Walter
Mildmay [Chancellor] made motion that as all they there met
30   together in peace and love so did wish they should so depart and
that no advantage should be taken of any words there past but all
to the best. After him Grimstone did the like, making motion also
that a collection should be made for the relief of the French
Church which was done, and amounted about £30; and that the
35   Queen might be moved for the recovery of Ireland into good
order, whereby again would grow to her an ease to all her
subjects; towards which her subjects gladly would contribute of
their goods another subsidy etc. . . .

    At length the speaker stood up, and he made the like requests of
40   love and amity as also craved the goodwill of every person there,
and that if he had slipped in anything they should impute it to his
ignorance and not to any wilfulness, and that he was and would
be pressed not only to do his best for that house, but also for
every one of them to his uttermost if he might stand them in
45   stead.

    At afternoon about five of the clock the Queen's Majesty came
to the higher house and going in to a several [i.e. separate] room
appointed for the purpose she apparelled herself in her royal robes
of Parliament and a coronet on her head, and then came in to the
50   higher house and sat in the seat of estate, and then all things being
settled the Speaker came, and being without the lowest bar at the
middle, after he had made his three obeisances, made his ovation
declaring how that the Common House of Parliament being
assembled by her commandment had condescended upon sundry
55   and diverse laws as well for and concerning religion as also for her
safety and for the common estate of the realm, which nevertheless
were no laws until that she had allowed and given her consent
thereunto, which done then were they laws and to be obeyed,
observed and kept as laws . . . . Then he declared of the goodwill
60   and hearty love the lower house bore unto her, and how that
freely without the denying of any one person or of any demand or
motion made they have given her a subsidy and two tens and
fifteenths. . . .

> *John Hooker's Journal in the House of Commons, 1571*, op cit,
> pp 488–9

Questions

a From the information given in extract *a*, state briefly the privileges of the House of Commons as its Elizabethan members believed them to be.

★ *b* What abuse of privilege did Arthur Hall and Edward Smalley perpetrate in 1576, in a way foreshadowed by the Lord Chancellor in extract *b*?

c Use extract *b* lines 14–22 to suggest what role Elizabeth wished for the Commons, and what her perception of 'freedom of speech' was.

★ *d* What matters had arisen 'the last time' (1566) that should make the queen wish for the Commons to be 'more quiet' (line 26)?

e What interests do the Commons of 1571 share with the Commons of 1601? (See Section 6*b*.)

f With reference to both extracts *a* and *b*, discuss the role of the Speaker in Elizabeth's parliaments.

(d) Peter Wentworth in the Commons, 8 February 1576

. . . Amongst other, Mr. Speaker, two things do great hurt in this place, of the which I do mean to speak. The one is a rumour which runs about the House, and this it is: 'take heed what you do: the Queen's Majesty likes not such a matter; whosoever
5 prefers it, she will be offended with him'. The other: sometimes a message is brought into the House, either of commanding or inhibiting, very injurious to the freedom of speech and consultation. I would to God, Mr. Speaker, that these two were buried in hell. I mean rumours and messages, for wicked undoubtedly they are;
10 the reason is the devil was the first author of them, from whom proceeds nothing but wickedness. . . .

Now the other was a message Mr. Speaker brought the last sessions into the House, that we should not deal in any matters of religion but first to receive from the bishops. Surely this was a
15 doleful message, for it was as much as to say, Sirs, ye shall not deal in God's causes, no, ye shall in no wise seek to advance His glory. . . .

It is a dangerous thing in a prince unkindly to abuse his or her nobility and people and it is a dangerous thing in a prince to
20 oppose or bend herself against her nobility and people. . . . And how could any prince more unkindly entreat, abuse, oppose herself against her nobility and people than her Majesty did the last Parliament? . . . And will not this her Majesty's handling, think you, Mr. Speaker, make cold dealing in any of her Majesty's
25 subjects toward her again? I fear it will. . . . And I beseech . . . God to endue her Majesty with His wisdom, whereby she may discern faithful advice from traitorous, sugared speeches, and to

send her Majesty a melting, yielding heart unto sound counsel,
that will may not stand for a reason; and then her Majesty will
30 stand when her enemies are fallen, for no estate can stand where
the prince will not be governed by advice. . . .

Sir Simonds D'Ewes, *The Journals of All the Parliaments
during the Reign of Queen Elizabeth*, pp 236–40

(e) Wentworth chastised

This day Mr. Treasurer, in the name of all the committees
yesterday appointed for the examination of Peter Wentworth,
burgess for Tregony, declared that all the said committees did
35 meet yesterday at afternoon, at the Star-Chamber, according to
their commission, and there examining the said Peter Wentworth,
touching the violent and wicked words yesterday pronounced by
him in this House touching the Queen's Majesty, made a collection
of the same words, which words, so collected, the said Peter
40 Wentworth did acknowledge and confess, and then did the same
Mr. Treasurer read to the House the said note of collection: which
being read, he declared further that the said Peter Wentworth,
being examined, what he could say for the extenuation of his said
fault and offence, could neither say any thing at all to that
45 purpose, neither yet did charge any other person as author of his
said speech; but did take all the burden thereof upon himself. And
so the said Mr. Treasurer thereupon moved for his punishment
and imprisonment in the Tower, as the House should think good,
and consider of: whereupon, after sundry disputations and
50 speeches, it was ordered, upon the question, that the said Peter
Wentworth should be committed close prisoner to the Tower, for
his said offence; there to remain until such time as this House
should have any further consideration of him. . . .

The Journal of the House of Commons, vol I, p 104

Questions

a To which M.P.s did Elizabeth entrust her 'rumours and
messages'?
b Whose influence over the queen and parliament does Wentworth
most resent? From what standpoint?
★ c Suggest why parliament resolved to discipline Wentworth
itself.
d Where towards the end of extract *e* is there a hint that
Wentworth was not without sympathisers in the House of
Commons?
★ e For how long did Wentworth remain in the Tower on this
occasion?

4   Star Chamber

There is yet in England another Court, of the which that I can
understand there is not the like in any other country. In the term-
time . . . every week once at the least (which is commonly on
Fridays and Wednesdays, and the next day after that the term does
5   end) the Lord Chancellor and the Lords and others of the Privy
Council so many as will, and other Lords and Barons which be
not of the Privy Council, and be in the town, and the judges of
England, specially the two chief judges, from nine of the clock till
it be eleven, do sit in a place which is called the Star-Chamber,
10   either because it is full of windows, or because at the first all the
roof thereof was decked with images of stars gilded. There is
plaints heard of riots . . . .

And further, because such things are not commonly done by
the mean men, but such as be of power and force, and be not to
15   be dealt withal of every man, nor of mean gentlemen: if the riot
be found and certified to the King's council, or if otherwise it be
complained of, the party is sent for, and he must appear in the
Star-Chamber . . .: for that is the effect of the court, to bridle
such stout noblemen or gentlemen which would offer wrong by
20   force to any manner men, and cannot be content to demand or
defend the right by order of law. This court began long before,
but took augmentation and authority at that time that Cardinal
Wolsey, Archbishop of York, was Chancellor of England, who of
some was thought to have first devised that court, because that he,
25   after some intermission by negligence of time, augmented the
authority of it . . . .

The judges of this court are the Lord Chancellor, the Lord
Treasurer, all the King's Majesty's Council, the barons of this land
. . . . The punishment most usual is imprisonment, pillory or
30   fine, and many times both fine and imprisonment . . . .

Sir Thomas Smith, *The Commonwealth of England* (1589),
Book III, Chapter 4, in G. W. Prothero, *Select Statutes*,
pp 180–1

Questions

a   From the evidence of the extract, suggest why the Court of
State Chamber was a more or less 'popular' court in Elizabeth's
reign.

★   b   Which other punishments, besides those cited, were available
to the Court? Which were not?

c   In what ways was the Court of Star Chamber more arbitrary
than a court of common law?

★   d   Section 3e provides evidence of other uses of the Star Chamber
room itself. Do you consider this might have confused
contemporaries about the scope of the Court of Star Chamber?

5 Shire Government

(a) . . . Over each of these shires in time of necessity is a several [i.e. separate] Lieutenant chosen under the prince, who, being a nobleman of calling, has almost regal authority over the same for the time being in many causes which do concern his office,
5 otherwise, it is governed by a sheriff . . . whose office is to gather up and bring his accounts into the exchequer, of the profits of his county received . . . .

In the election also of these magistrates, diverse able persons, as well for wealth as wisdom, are named by the commons at a time
10 and place appointed for their choice, whose names being delivered to the prince, he forthwith picks some such one of them as he pleases to assign to that office, to whom he commits the charge of the county and who hereupon is sheriff of that shire for one whole year, or until a new be chosen. The sheriff also has his undersheriff
15 . . . . There are likewise under him certain bailiffs, whose office is to serve and return such writs and processes as are directed to them from the high sheriff; to make seizure of the goods and chattels and arrest the bodies of such as do offend, presenting either their persons to him, or at the leastwise taking sufficient
20 bond or other assurance of them for their dutiful appearance, at an appointed time, when the sheriff by order of law ought to present them to the judges according to his charge. In every hundred also are one or more high constables . . . .

In each county likewise are sundry law days held at their
25 appointed seasons, of which some retain the old Saxon name and are called mootlaw . . . . They have, finally, their quarter sessions, wherein they are assisted by the justices and gentlemen of the country, and twice in the year jail delivery, at which time the judges ride about in their circuits into every several county . . .
30 and minister the laws of the realm with great solemnity and justice . . . .

Besides these officers afore mentioned, there are sundry other in every county, as coroners, whose duty is to enquire of such as come to their death by violence, to attach and present the pleas of
35 the Crown, to make enquiry of treasurer found etc. There are diverse also of the best learned of the law, beside sundry gentlemen, where the number of lawyers will not suffice (and whose revenues do amount to above £20 by the year) appointed by especial commission from the prince to look to the good
40 government of her subjects in the counties where they dwell. And of these the least skilful in the law are of the peace, the other both of the peace and quorum, otherwise called of 'oyer and determiner' [to hear and determine], so that the first have authority only to

45 hear, the others to hear and determine such matters as are brought
to their presence . . . .
William Harrison, *The Description of England* (1577), ed.
Georges Edelen (Cornell U.P., 1968), pp 88–92

Questions

★ a In which year did 'time of necessity' (line 1) give way to the
appointment of permanent Lords Lieutenant?
b What were the tasks of the sheriff?
c What varieties of judges and justices does Harrison list?
d In what ways was the influence of land and property owners
over local government and justice preserved?

(b) (The) President [Earl of Sussex] and Council of the North 'to
the Queen. According to your commission and instructions, we
have kept one sitting here at York, for administration of justice,
from 9th to 24th May, and ordered all the causes, by decrees, by
5 dismissals, or by remitting to other courts for lack of proof etc.
We then kept a session of oyer and terminer; at the end we
conferred with the justices of peace in the county for its good
order, and finding great quiet and content by the good execution
of the statute for vagabonds, we have taken order that once in
10 every month there shall be a secret search for that purpose
throughout the shire, and certificates sent us, until next November.
We find no disorders at present fit to be advertised. For the ease
and good order of the people upon the Borders, we have appointed
a sitting at Newcastle on 11th July, and a session of oyer and
15 terminer there; and after to consider of the decay of houses and
tillage and enclosures upon the Borders, and of all other matters
contained in your instructions.
(Enclosed: account of 84 new cases adjudicated upon
115 old cases adjudicated upon
20 Prisoners tried at oyer and terminer:
5 executed (i.e. convicted and sentenced)
1 reprieved
2 acquitted by verdict
10 acquitted by proclamation
25 5 stayed till next jail delivery
2 punished as vagabonds.)
26 May 1569
Calendar of State Papers Domestic, Addenda, 1566–1579, p 77

Questions

a Describe, using the information given in the extract, how the
Council of the North kept communications open from the top
to the bottom of the ladder of government.

b Cite two subjects of recent legislation in which the local administrators here took an interest.

★ *c* In the light of subsequent events, comments on lines 8 (and finding . . . content) and 11.

6 Money

(a) Methods for levy of money [Lord Burghley?]

[1588] A consideration of diverse things that do belong to the execution of that contribution which the necessity of this present time does require.

5 First: there can be no motion nor authority for levies of money but by especial commission from her Majesty, wherein seeing this is not meant to be an imposition but a trial of men's affection, there is especially to be considered who shall be her Majesty's ministers to handle this, and from what sort and kind of subjects

10 the contributions are to be drawn. Because the great part of the livings and revenues in England are in the hands of the Spirituality, her Majesty must write letters to the Metropolitans of Canterbury and York, commanding them to write to all bishops to consider the names of all within their diocese that are able to yield any

15 manner of contribution, none to be dealt with but such as have £20 yearly to live on . . . .

In these letters to the clergy, the present necessity is to be remembered; the charge her Majesty has been and is daily out of her own coffers; the quiet they enjoy; the former precedents of

20 contributions by men of their function; that they are fought for while they sit quiet; that the case of the rebellion in Ireland is pretended for extirpation of religion, and that their example and persuasion is most forcible and necessary . . . .

Think of a good Treasurer.

25 Persons for raising the contributions of the Laity:

For the City of London, letters to the Lord Mayor and Aldermen . . . .

The like to all cities that are counties within themselves . . . .

Note that of all sorts of dwellers in the country, the cornmen

30 are of best ability [added note] (maltmen, sheepmasters, moneymen, graziers).

Persons of several callings, all officers and ministers in Courts of Justice . . . all officers under the Earl Marshal of England, of the Admiralty, the Ordnance; all judges, sergeants, practisers at

35 Law, heads of Colleges and Halls, all officers of the customs, all merchant strangers [i.e. foreigners] . . . .

Gentlemen that have recusants to their wives.

If this be well conducted, and that selected persons prepare the way to others, all men will fall to contribute out of one affection

40 or other, as well as they did when the like benevolence was
termed 'nolens, volens' [willy-nilly: i.e. compulsory].

Calendar of the MSS of the Marquis of Salisbury, vol XIII,
Addenda, p 391

Questions

★ *a* Comment on the phrase 'the necessity of this present time'
(lines 2–3).

b Identity *two* separate lines where it is indicated that money is to
be raised by *voluntary* contributions.

c What skills might 'ministers to handle this' need (line 9)?

★ *d* Comment on the statement, 'the great part of the livings and
revenues in England are in the hands of the Spirituality' (lines
10–11).

e In what different ways are religious consciences and sus-
ceptibilities put under pressure to contribute?

f What does this extract suggest about Elizabethan governments'
facilities for raising money?

(b) An Act for the granting of four entire subsidies and eight fifteenths and tenths granted by the temporalty, 1601

Most excellent and most gracious Sovereign, where we your
Majesty's humble, faithful and loving subjects being here (by your
authority) assembled . . . have entered into due consideration of
the great and weighty causes which ought at this time, more than

5 at any other time, to stir up the hearts of all that are either well
affected in religion towards God, loyalty towards you their dear
sovereign, or care of their safety and their posterity's, to consult
timely and provide effectually for all such means as are or may be
necessary to preserve both you and us from those apparent dangers

10 whereinto this state may fall through lack of so much care and
providence . . . .
And where it is apparent to all the world that if your Majesty
had not exhausted the greatest portion of your private treasures,
besides all other means derived from our dutiful affections, as well

15 in making timely provision of all things necessary for your navy
and army royal, as in maintaining and using the same . . . that we
should long before this day have been exposed to the danger of
many sudden and dangerous attempts of our enemies . . . . And,
seeing also that at this present time your Highness has been put to

20 inestimable charge in the necessary prosecution of an unnatural
rebellion within your Highness's realm of Ireland, daily fed by
foreign enemies . . . .
In which consideration, and many others needless to repeat, we
have thought ourselves bound in thankfulness to God to you, and

25   to your Majesty for ourselves, who feel the happiness of your
       most gracious clemency and justice at home, under your happy
       and politic government daily multiplied unto us (beyond the
       example of all ages) to prepare and make not only our persons
       ready to withstand, resist and subdue the force and puissance of
30   our enemies (be they never so potent), but also to present unto
       you four subsidies and eight fifteenths and tenths, thereby to make
       up some such portion of treasure as may (in some sort) supply the
       great and inestimable charges which you our most gracious and
       dread Sovereign have and daily must sustain. . . .

       43 Elizabeth c.18 (1601), *Statutes of the Realm*, vol IV,
       Part II, pp 991–2

Questions

★   *a*   What was the customary level of taxation at the start of
         Elizabeth's reign? Give as many reasons as you can why the
         level had increased so much by 1601.

★   *b*   What were the sources of Elizabeth's 'private treasures' (line 13)?
         Did she accumulate or dissipate her own finances? Give reasons
         for your answer.

    c   What does the extract suggest to us about the political and
         religious temper of parliament in 1601?

VII   'A most beautiful and sweet country' – Scotland and Ireland

Introduction

In studying Elizabethan Scotland and Ireland we must first forget what we already know; that the reign ended with the military pacification of Ireland and the peaceful accession of James VI to the throne of England. The relations between the peoples of England, Ireland and Scotland, rulers and commons alike, are shot through with anxiety and suspicion, breaking out at times into open warfare.

The significance of Scotland gradually changes during the reign from the ancient preoccupation with the northern border and fears of the 'Auld Alliance' with France, which are still uppermost in the crisis of 1559–1560, to concern about the succession and the dubious positions, first of Mary Queen of Scots, and later of James VI. In their correspondence James and Elizabeth, whether at one or at odds, whether giving expression to the warmth of their friendship or frankly stating their grievances, communicate with an air of desperation that arises because they depend on each other and mistrust each other at one and the same time.

In Ireland the Crown of England was notionally sovereign, and this sovereignty gives the 'Irish problem', from the English point of view, characteristics of the problems of the north of England writ large. In Ireland as in the north there are religious alienation, ancient loyalties to a kind of 'bastard feudalism', foreign intervention and an inadequate military response born of money problems. Morton in his study of Elizabethan Ireland happily refers to Tyrone and O'Donnell in 1601 as 'the northern earls'. From the Irish point of view the question is of religion, of self-determination and of the preservation of Irish institutions such as Brehon Law and succession by 'tanistry'.

The miseries of inconclusive warfare during Elizabeth's reign are open to question. Black, in his Oxford History volume, suggests that there is a balance sheet including economic stimulation of Ireland by the money spent there on military activities.

This chapter cannot be comprehensive. I have chosen, to stand for all the campaigns in Elizabethan Ireland, the climax at Kinsale in 1601–2.

1 Scotland – the Reformation

(a) John Knox and the congregation

1559: Now the professors of the Protestants' religion in Scotland,
who had taken upon themselves the name of the Congregation
(being persuaded by some importune ministers, and especially by
Knox, a most fervent impugner of the Queen's authority, that it
5 was the duty of the Nobility and Estates by their own authority to
abolish idolatry, and by force to reduce princes within the prescript
of the Laws), had refused to yield obedience to the Regent the
Queen's Mother, a most modest Matron, changed religion,
tumultuously firing and sacking religious places, and had drawn
10 to their party Hamilton, Duke of Châtelherault . . . and many of the
chief nobility, allured with the hope of the revenues of the Church:
insomuch as they seemed to the Lady Regent and the French soldiers
that served in Scotland, not to aim at Religion, but to attempt a flat
revolt: and James, Prior of St. Andrews, the Queen's base brother
15 (who was afterwards Earl of Murray), the ringleader amongst them,
was by them [the French] accused for affecting the crown against his
sister. He labours to remove a suspicion, most religiously protesting
that he sought nothing else but God's glory and the liberty of his
country, and could not but sorrowfully bewail the suppressing
20 thereof by the Lady Regent and the French.

The Masters of the Congregation began now to complain to
Queen Elizabeth, by William Maitland of Lethington, Lord
Secretary, in a lamentable oration, to wit, that from the time the
Queen of Scots was married to the Dauphin, the government of
25 the kingdom was changed, foreign soldiers wasted all places, the
highest offices of the kingdom were bestowed upon Frenchmen,
the castles and strongholds delivered into their hands and the
purer money of the realm debased for their gain, and that by these
and such like cunning practices, the French did craftily make
30 themselves way to seize upon the kingdom of Scotland, if anything
should befall the Queen other than well. Cecil . . . dealt by Henry
Percy, Earl afterwards of Northumberland, that he might
understand what was the scope which these Masters of the
Congregation proposed to themselves, by what means they were
35 able to compass that they sought, and (if at any time they were
aided) upon what conditions amity might grow between the two
kingdoms. They answer with eyes lifted up to heaven, that they
have no other aim but to advance the glory of Jesus Christ, and
the sincere preaching of God's Word, to root out superstitions and
40 idolatry, to restrain the fury of their persecutors and preserve their
ancient liberty. . . .

William Camden, *The History of the Most Renowned and
Victorious Princess Elizabeth* (1630), pp 34–5

(b) James VI's Coronation Oath, 1567

Because that the increase of virtue, and suppressing of idolatry, craves that the Prince and the People be of one perfect religion, which of God's mercy is now presently professed within this
45 realm, therefore it is statute and ordained . . . that all Kings and Princes, or Magistrates whatsoever holding their place, which hereafter in any time shall happen to reign and bear rule over this Realm, at the time of their coronation, and receipt of their princely authority make their faithful promise, by oath, in presence of the
50 eternal God, that during the whole course of their life they shall serve the same eternal God to the uttermost of their power, according as He has required in His most holy word, revealed and contained in the New and Old Testaments. And according to the same word, shall maintain the true Religion of Jesus Christ, the
55 preaching of His Holy Word, and due and right administration of the Sacraments now received and preached within this Realm. And shall abolish and stand against all false religion contrary to the same. And shall rule the people committed to their charge according to the will and command of God, revealed in his
60 aforesaid word and according to the Lovable Laws and constitutions received in this Realm, no wise repugnant to the said word of the eternal God. And shall procure to the uttermost of their power, to the Kirk of God, and all Christian people, true and perfect peace in all time coming. The rights, and rents, with all just privileges of
65 the Crown of Scotland to preserve and keep inviolate, neither shall they transfer nor alienate the same. They shall forbid and repress, in all estates and degrees, rife, oppression and all kind of wrong. In all judgments they shall command and procure that Justice and equity be kept to all creatures, without exception as the
70 Lord and Father of all mercies be merciful to them. And out of their lands and empire they be careful to root out all heretics and enemies to the true worship of God, that shall be convicted by the true Kirk of God of the aforesaid crimes. And that they shall faithfully affirm the things above written by their solemn oath.

The Acts of the Parliaments of Scotland III, 23 c.8

Questions

★ *a* Why was Knox regarded as an 'impugner of the Queen's authority' (line 4)?

 b According to Camden, what diverse motivations led to the rebellion of the Congregation?

★ *c* With reference to extracts *a* and *b*, describe the points of similarity and difference between the Reformations in Scotland and England. In particular, what were the relationships of the monarchs to the church?

★ *d* How was the crisis of 1559–60 settled? Was this the end of English and French intervention in Scotland in Elizabeth's reign?

2 Scotland – Mary, James and Elizabeth

(a) *Mary's offences and fate*

There has not happened since the memory of man, nor, perhaps, in any age beyond, so strange a case on every behalf to be considered, as this of that unfortunate Lady the late Scottish Queen. . . .

5   And first, it is not to be denied that the said unfortunate Lady, the Scottish Queen, entering into this realm of England upon the sudden with certain troops of horsemen, . . . her purpose and determination not before known, and being secretly harboured in places of those parts very suspicious or nothing seemly or
10   convenient for so great a personage, the Warden of her Majesty's borders being informed thereof resorted to her with all possible speed, and as became him, in all courteous and dutiful manner, entreated the said Queen to be contented to change her lodging to some more convenient and commodious place at his appointment,
15   and that it would please her there to stay herself till the Queen's Majesty (our sovereign Lady) might be advertised of her arrival, and her pleasure known back again. . . .

But they on the other side will perchance say, that the said Lady's restraint continued many years longer than it ought to have
20   done, and that to win her liberty by any possible means or device, she ought to be holden excused. . . .

But the said Scottish Queen's malice and treasons were not hidden from the world, either before she came into the realm or since. Being, therefore, by the providence of God, fallen upon the
25   person and place that have power over her life, with lawful authority to decide right and revenge their own injuries, as well by civil judgment as by the sword . . . her Majesty may no doubt use either of them, at her election and good pleasure, without injustice. . . .

30   But the said most unfortunate and unquiet minded Queen, intending nothing less than perfect amity, trifled of her accord, and even in the prime of her Majesty's greatest and most honourable entreaty of her person, caused some of her subjects, one Harvey by name, a Scottish priest remaining with the Bishop
35   of Ross, her Ambassador liegier [resident] here in England, to prefer to the print a certain seditious pamphlet declaring her title to the crown of England; a matter of so great a danger to the state (though in appearance she seemed to shoot but at the next

40 succession) that the books were speedily suppressed, the priest sent to prison, and the printer well punished for his labour. . . .

And so, by the Laws of England, in the highest degree of honour and justice, the said unfortunate Queen was condemned to die, and suffered upon the 8th day of February, 1586 [1587 New Style], at Fotheringay Castle, in the County of Northampton. . . .

A Justification of Queen Elizabeth, in Relation to the Affair of Mary Queen of Scots, eds A. J. Crosby and J. Bruce (Camden Society, 1867), pp 67, 86, 99, 106, 108, 112

(b) The fury of the Scots

45 The next year, which was 1586, was the Queen of Scots' beheading [February 1587 N.S., February 1586 O.S.]. I lived in court, had small means of my friends; yet God so blessed me that I was ever able to keep company with the best. . . . At which time (few or none in court being willing to undertake that journey) her Majesty
50 sent me to the King of Scots, to make known her innocence of her sister's [i.e. cousin's] death, with letters of credence from herself to assure all that I should affirm.

I was [i.e. would have been] waylaid in Scotland, if I had gone in, to have been murdered; but the King's Majesty, knowing the
55 disposition of his people, and the fury they were in, sent to me to Berwick, to let me know that no power of his could warrant my life at that time; therefore, to prevent further mischief, he would send me no convoy, but would send two of his Council to the boundary, to receive my letters, or what other message I had to
60 deliver. . . .

I was commanded to accept of the King's offer. Sir George Home and the Master of Melvin met me at the boundary, where I delivered my message in writing, and my letters from the Queen to the King, and then presently to court where I had thanks of her
65 Majesty for what I had done.

The Memoirs of Robert Carey, ed. F. H. Mares (1972), p 7

(c) Elizabeth excuses herself

Elizabeth to James VI: February 1587

Be not carried away, my dear brother, with the lewd persuasions of such as, instead of informing you of my too needful and helpless cause of defending the breath that God has given me, to
70 be better spent than spilt by the bloody invention of traitor's hands, may perhaps make you believe, that either [Mary's] offence was not so great, or if that cannot serve them, . . . yet the while make that her life may be saved and mine safe, which would God were true, for when you make view of my long danger endured
75 these four – well nigh five – months' time to make a taste [test?] of the greater wits amongst my own, and then of [the] French, and

last[ly] of you, you will grant with me, that if need were not more than my malice she should not have her merit.

. . . Your commissioners tell me that I may trust her in the
80 hand of some indifferent [i.e. neutral] prince, and have all her cousins and allies promise she will no more seek my ruin. . . . Suppose you me mad to trust my life in another's hand and send it out of my own? . . . Let your councillors, for your honour, discharge their duty so much to you as to declare the absurdity of
85 such an offer. . . .

And now to conclude. Make account, I pray you, of my firm friendship, love and care, of which you may make sure account, as one that never minds to fail from my word, nor swerve from our league, but will increase by all good means, any action that
90 may make true show of my stable amity. . . .

James VI to Elizabeth: March 1587

Madame and dearest sister, whereas by your letter and bearer, Robert Carey, your servant and ambassador, you purge yourself of yon unhappy fact. As, on the one part, considering your rank
95 and sex, consanguinity [kinship] and long-professed goodwill to the defunct [Mary], together with your many and solemn attestations of your innocence, I dare not wrong you so far as not to judge of your unspotted part therein, so, on the other side, I wish that your honourable behaviour in all times hereafter may
100 fully persuade the whole world of the same. And, as for my part, I look that you will give me at this time such a full satisfaction, in all respects, as shall be a means to strengthen and unite this isle, establish and maintain the true religion, and oblige me to be, as of before I was, your most loving . . . .

Letters of Queen Elizabeth and King James VI of Scotland, ed. J. Bruce (Camden Society, 1849), pp 43–6

Questions

★ *a* Write a short account of Mary's 'malice and treasons' against Elizabeth (line 22).
b What other offences does the pamphleteer lay to her charge?
c What is the tone of the correspondence between James and Elizabeth on either side?
d Where in his letter does James hint at the truth of Robert Carey's remarks about the fury of the Scots people?
★ *e* Discuss the options concerning Mary Queen of Scots from Elizabeth's point of view.

(d) A cordial correspondence

King James VI of Scotland to Queen Elizabeth: 4 August 1588

In times of straits true friends are best tried . . . and so this time must move me to utter my zeal to the religion and how near a

kinsman and neighbour I find myself to you and your country.
For this effect then have I sent you this present hereby to offer to
you my forces, my person and all that I may command to be
employed against yon strangers in whatsoever fashion and by
whatsoever means as may best serve for the defence of your
country. Wherein I promise to behave myself not as a stranger and
foreign prince but as your natural son and compatriot of your
country in all respects . . . .

    Queen Elizabeth to King James VI of Scotland: 8 October 1588

    Albeit, my dear brother, the mighty malice and huge armies of
my hateful enemies and causeless foes have apparently spit out
their venomous poison and mortal hate; yet, through God's
goodness, our power so weakened their pride, [and] cut off their
numbers at the first that they ran away to their further overthrow.
And so mightily has our God wrought for our innocency that
places of their greatest trust have turned to prosecute them
most. . . . Among the rest of their succours I suppose your realm
to have been supposed not to have been least willing nor the most
unready to answer their trust, which I doubt not had answered
their expectations if your natural affection towards me and regard
of our strait amity had not impeached their landing. . . .

    Calendar of the MSS of the Marquis of Salisbury, vol XIII,
Addenda, pp 380, 384

(e) The other side of the coin

Ferdinand I, Grand Duke of Tuscany, to James VI [via Sir Michael
Balfour, James's envoy] 1599

    1. We do acknowledge the King's title and right to be most just
and nearest to the Crown of England.

    2. It is most necessary and convenient that the King should with
all princes his friends, alliances and confederates, renew and
establish his friendship. But it is to be observed that he treat with
them both warily and secretly, and especially in his dealing with
the King of Spain, that the Queen of England may not be induced
to have any suspicion, or that she may not hereby be moved to
think that he should in any way practise the shortening of her life.

    3. The King shall do most wisely to dissimulate with Ireland
and not to make show of any friendship that he has with them
during the Queen's life.

    4. It is most necessary that the King should make a friendship
with the Pope, [without] whom goodly I do not see how he can
be assisted by princes Catholic. . . .

    5. It is requisite to review the old alliance with France, and
make great friendship with the King, for putting further off his
head any jealousy that he may have of your greatness, and in
giving him assurance that you will not, nor [intend] ever to
pursue any title that the Kings of England have to France.

6. It is most requisite and necessary that when God calls the Queen of England, that the King should immediately enter in that country, having an open and ready way, so strongly that no
50 enemy may resist him, and for this effect let the King daily and hourly furnish himself of all things necessary to doubly further such an enterprise. . . .

7. It pleases us the faction that the King has in England but that they have [enough] spirits or force to do the King's turn we do
55 not see it: always let them be entertained and dealt with privily, to see if they can bring in discredit and to confusion his unfriends.

8. So great is the goodwill that the Earl of Essex has conquest of the soldiers and bravest spirits of England, and so liberal and beneficial has he been and is he towards them, that his force and
60 power is more to be thought of [than] any in these parts, but that any ways goodly he may pretend any title or right to the throne, except he come to [Arabella Stuart, daughter of Charles Earl of Lennox] we do not see it. Wherefore it [is] most necessary that he be dealt with and large offers made to him etc.

65 9. If the King cannot assuredly by himself, by me he may etc. Note the good opinion that the Catholics have of the Earl.

It is requisite to use diligence in this because the greatest competitor minds by this way he make himself an easier access to that Crown.

> *Negotiations between King James VI and Ferdinand I*, No VI, in
> *A Source Book of Scottish History*, vol III, 1567–1707, eds
> W. G. Dickinson and G. Donaldson (1954), pp. 451–3

Questions

a What were James's interests in the success or failure of the Spanish Armada?
★ b Besides Scotland, which other 'places of their greatest trust . . . turned to prosecute them most' (lines 19–20)?
c Who other than Ferdinand of Tuscany might have coloured the points made in extract *e*?
d How was the difficulty in Point 8 removed before Elizabeth's death?
e Who do you suppose was the 'greatest competitor' (lines 67–68)?
★ f How far do extracts *d* and *e*, and James's behaviour towards England between 1588 and 1603, bear out Thomas Randolph's remark that 'he hath need of a long spoon that sups with the Devil'?
★ g What did English people have to hope for, and to fear, from James VI's accession to the English throne?

3 Ireland – Analysis

(a) Elizabeth sows and reaps rebellion

The Irish action we may call a malady, and a consumption of
[Elizabeth's] times, for it accompanied her to her end, and it was
of so profuse and vast an expense, that it drew near unto a
distemperature of state, and of passion in herself, for, towards her
5   last, she grew somewhat hard to please, her armies being
accustomed to prosperity, and the Irish prosecution not answering
her expectation, and her wonted success; for it was a good while
an unthrifty and inauspicious war, which did much disturb and
mislead her judgement; and the more, for that it was a precedent
10 taken out of her own pattern.

For as the Queen, by way of division, had at her coming to the
crown, supported the revolted states of Holland, so did the King
of Spain turn the trick upon herself, towards her going out, by
cherishing the Irish Rebellion.

> Sir Robert Naunton, *Fragmenta Regalia* (1641), (Edward
> Jeffery, 1797), p 86

(b) Urban financial pleas

15 Patrick Galway, Agent for the City of Cork, to Sir Robert Cecil
(1586?)

The city for ten or twelve years past has been charged with the
maintenance of Garrisons and companies of Soldiers, and has
received very little recompense, having for years since lost sundry
20 of the captains' bills amounting to £300 or £400. Though greatly
impoverished of late by casualty of fire and spoil of pirates at sea,
they are yet continually charged with the like. The Council of
Ireland has sent letters to the Council for the payment to suppliants
of £222 5s 4d. upon warrants from Sir William Russell and docket
25 from Sir Henry Wallop, Treasurer of Ireland.

> *Calendar of the MSS of the Marquis of Salisbury*, op cit, p 325

(c) Rural financial pleas

In this time [1573], Sir Henry Sidney being Lord Deputy of the
country, finding themselves grieved with great unreasonable
charges, they complained to the Lord Deputy thereof, but finding
not such redress as they liked of at his hand nor the Council's, sent
30 Barnaby Scorlock, a man of 60 years old, well learned in the
Laws, Richard Netterfield, a man of best experience in the
country's doings, and one Harry Bernell, a wise and learned man
in the Laws, to show their griefs to the Queen's Majesty: and
being there before her Majesty's Council, were committed to
35 close prison in the Fleet, for that they spoke against the Queen's

prerogative, as it was supposed. But truly they never spoke nor thought anything against the prerogative, but declared the charges that were levied upon the country by reason of the cess [customary Irish taxation] and slack payment, which continued these 28 years

40 past; by reason thereof the realm was utterly decayed and impoverished. . . .

[Twelve Lords and gentlemen of the Pale] were committed to the [Dublin] Castle, where . . . they rested [stayed] twelve weeks or more. . . .

45 In this time the whole cess was reared upon the ploughland[s]. which came to twelve pounds sterling upon the ploughland: and another cess was levied in Connaught, another cess in Munster and another cess upon the gentlemen's freedoms. . . .

The Book of Howth, Calendar of the Carew MSS, pp 213–14

Questions

★ *a* Explain the basis and workings of cess (lines 38–48).

    b Where did the costs of Elizabeth's campaigns in Ireland fall? (See also Chapter 6, Section 6.)

★ *c* Develop and criticise Naunton's comparison between Ireland and the Netherlands.

(d) Irish remedies

The Earl of Tyrone to Don Carolo

I have been informed by the bearer of this that you have written to me, but your letter has not yet reached my hands. I was confident that I should not in vain appeal to you for aid. The faith

5 might be re-established in Ireland within one year, if the King of Spain would send only 3000 soldiers. All the heretics would disappear, and no other sovereign would be recognised than the King Catholic. Both I and O'Donnell have besought him to succour the Church. Pray second our petition. If we obtain

10 positive assurance of succour from the King, we will make no peace with the heretics. We have written frequently, but are afraid none of our letters have reached the King, as he has returned us no answer [The King did reply in January 1596]. The bearer, a man of pious zeal, has undertaken this perilous mission.

15 5 Cal. Octobris [27 September] [1595]

Signed: Amicus tuus ignotus [your unknown friend] – O'Neill.

Countersigned: Francis Montfort.

'Intercepted and received the 29 September from the hands of Piers O'Cullen.'

Calendar of the Carew MSS 1589–1600, pp 122–3

(e) A sort of normality

20 Sir George Carew to Sir Thomas Heneage, 1588

Being in a place where I cannot express by service the unfeigned goodwill I bear to you, I pray you to accept from time to time a few lines imparting to you the state of this commonwealth, which I find reduced at present to a superficial kind of peace, and may so

25 continue till foreign powers or the brood of rebels be grown in strength sufficient to infringe it. It is embraced by these people more from policy than allegiance. The principal and special point which ties men to do obedience, to wit, the knowledge of God, and the preaching of His Word, is by the pastors neglected, and

30 by the people rejected. Concerning politic government, every governor for his time makes fair weather, like a bad physician qualifying, not curing, the disease. If diligence were used to reform with sharpness and cherish with reward, this people would be brought to know God and obey her Majesty. No care has been

35 used to foster arts, liberal or mechanical; and all kinds of traffic, as marts, fairs and the like, which enrich a commonwealth by making men industrious, are little followed: errors which, whilst the memory of the late evils is fresh, might be easily redressed. . . .

Calendar of the Carew MSS, 1575–1588, pp 468–9

(f) English remedies

Suggestions for the Government of Ireland [Lord Mountjoy, 1602]

40 . . . Towards the recovery of the hearts of the people there is but one means 'In rerum natura' [in the nature of things]: 1. Religion. 2. Justice and Protection. 3. Obligation and Reward.

For religion, to speak first of piety and then of policy. All divines do agree that if conscience be to be forced at all (wherein

45 they differ), yet two things must precede their enforcement: the one, means of instruction; the other, time of operation; neither of which they have yet had. . . .

For policy, there is no doubt but to wrestle with them now is directly opposite to their reclaim and cannot but continue their

50 alienation of mind from the Government. Therefore a toleration of religion at first (for a time not definite) except in some principal towns and precincts, after the manner of some French edicts, seems to me to be a matter warrantable by religion, and is policy of absolute necessity, and the hesitation on this part has I think

55 been a great casting back of affairs there. Neither if any English Papist or recusant shall for liberty of his conscience transfer his family and fortunes thither do I hold it a matter of danger, but rather an expedient to draw on undertaking and further population. But there would go hand in hand with this some course of

60 advancing religion where the people is capable thereof, as the sending over of some good preachers, specially of that sort which

are vehement and zealous persuaders and not scholastical, to be
resident in the principal towns, endowing them with some stipend
out of her Majesty's revenues as her Majesty has most religiously
65 and graciously done in Lancashire, and the recontinuing and
replenishing the college begun at Dublin, the placing of good men
to be bishops, etc. . . .

For justice, the barbarism and desolation of that country
considered, it is not possible they should find any sweetness at all
70 of it in case it be . . . formal and fetched far off from the State . . .
and therefore there must be an interim in which the justice must
be only summary, because it is fit and safe for a time the country
be participate of a 'martial' government. . . .

For obligation and reward, it is true, no doubt, which was
75 anciently said, that a State is contained in two words; 'praemium'
[reward] and 'poena' [penalty], and I am persuaded if a penny in
the pound which has been spent in 'poena' . . . had been spent in
'praemis', that is, in rewarding and contenting, things had never
grown to this extremity. The keeping of the principal persons
80 Irish in terms of contentment and without just particular of
complaint . . . is one of the best medicines of that estate.

For plantations and buildings, I do find it strange that in the last
plot for the population of Munster there were limitations how
much in demesne and how much in farm and tenancy, how many
85 buildings should be erected, how many Irish in mixture should be
admitted. . . .

> Calendar of the MSS of the Marquis of Salisbury, vol XIV,
> Addenda, pp 239–41

Questions

  a What does Tyrone claim to be fighting for?

★ *b* In the light of the events of 1596–1602, was Tyrone's claim
about Spanish help realistic?

  c In what way does the fate of this letter bear out Tyrone's
anxieties about his correspondence?

  d Which suggestions do Carew and Mountjoy make in common?
(Carew's suggestions are implied rather than expressed.)

  e What evidence is there that 'plantation' is a higher priority than
conversion in Mountjoy's scheme?

★ *f* What level of success had attended plantation in Ireland during
Elizabeth's reign?

★ *g* What was 'the college begun at Dublin' (line 66)?

4   Ireland – War and Truce

(a) The State of Ireland, September 1595

Ulster. . . . . Sir John Norris, Lord General of her Majesty's forces here, being coming from Armagh with her Majesty's army then with him from the victualling of the garrison there, he was encountered with the traitor Earl of Tyrone and the northern
5   rebels in that part of Ulster where the traitorous Earl lies. In which conflict Sir John Norris's horse was shot in four times and himself shot in twice with bullet; viz; once in the arm, and the other time in the lower part of the belly glancing. The charge was upon the rearward, where he, Sir Thomas Norris and all the brave
10   men, horse and foot, were. The traitors took them upon great advantage by a woodside, suffering the forward and the battle [i.e. the main body] to pass. The General, perceiving his horse thus hurt to faint under him, and being himself hurt as aforesaid, told his brother Sir Thomas Norris, 'I have,' quoth he, 'a lady's hurt. I
15   pray, brother make this place good if you love me, and I will new horse myself and return presently; and I pray charge home'. With that Sir Thomas, with a brave troop of horsemen, one hundred of those that be under the Lord General charged, in which charge Sir Thomas was shot through the left thigh, and lost about nine of his
20   horsemen and some few horse in that skirmish. We lost in all about thirty, and the traitors lost their found dead sixty. In the end they fled, and the General kept the field all night. . . .

Connaught. . . . . A great part of that province have of late revolted and been in actual rebellion. . . . O'Donnell was in that
25   province of late, and Sir Richard [Bingham] thought to have intercepted him on his way homeward, but by reason he marched day and night and hasted away, and for that our forces came hence but then, and went a long journey, and being before wearied, could not march so fast for weariness, and so O'Donnell
30   escaped. . . .

Munster. . . . . that province is very quiet.

Leinster. . . . . Here was one Fitz McHugh, a base fellow who has been these thirty years a great disturber of those parts, who dwelled within twenty-four miles of Dublin. A sharp prosecution
35   has been made against him, and he, flying still to the woods and bogs, will never fight, but burn villages and murder. . . .

> *Trevelyan Papers*, Part II, ed. J. Payne Collier (Camden Society, 1863), p 94

Questions

a   What light does this extract shed on Irish methods of warfare?
b   What difficulties did the English face in responding to these methods? What difficulties of supply and reinforcement did they face?

(b) The Earl of Essex and Tyrone

7 September 1599

My Lord Lieutenant General of the Kingdom of Ireland [began?] his march into the north part of the realm, whereas my Lord was met by two messengers sent from the Earl Tyrone. The force of their message was that the Earl Tyrone would earnestly entreat his Lord to parley with him, which at the first my Lord General refused, bidding him battle; but the Earl of Tyrone desired that, of his honourable favour, his Lordship would hear him first speak. They were distant between two hills very high, both their forces being, one under the one side of the one hill, and the other on the other hill, the two hills were some two miles distant asunder [the place was Aclint Ford, Louth-Monaghan border]. My Lord General came riding from his forces down, and the Earl Tyrone in like sort, and before he came near my Lord General by twelve score paces he was uncovered; and after he had done his humble duty to my Lord General, he began as follows;

'My honourable good Lord, since it is not unknown unto your Lordship how I married the sister of Sir Henry Bagenal, and living together, because I did affect two other gentlewomen, she grew in dislike with me, forsook me, and went unto her brother to complain upon me to the Council of Ireland, and did exhibit articles against me. Upon this they sent for me; and because I came not at their first sending, they proclaimed me a traitor, before I never meant to go out [i.e. rebel] and so then I had no other remedy but to go out to save my head; and so ever since I have been in this rebellion; and never since has there been, until the coming of your Lordship, any Deputy that I did dare to put my life into his hands; but, my honourable good Lord, my love to my dread the Queen's Majesty, and love I did bear unto your honourable father deceased, which was such as shall never be put out of my breast. . . . By [my] hand I swear what your Lordship shall think fit for me to do or undergo I will, and for ever hereafter will be a most true and loyal subject, and during my life I nor none of my followers shall hold up hand against your Lordship except it be to save my head . . . .'

Unto whose speeches my Lord General answered;

'If I were sure you would not violate your oath, and promise as heretofore you have already done, I would be very well content to speak to the Queen's Majesty, my mistress, for you; and, upon hope hereof, I will send my messengers to you with articles, the which, if you will subscribe unto, and send me in pledges for the performance thereof, I will send them to the Queen's Majesty, and will speak for you to have mercy. . . .'

Trevelyan Papers, op cit, pp 101–3

Questions

a Compare this extract with Chapter 1, Section 9. Do you think that the Irish rebels' motives are adequately represented in English documents by these personal excuses?

★ *b* What ills arose for Essex from his having negotiated with Tyrone without witnesses? (See Chapter 5, Section 5*b*.)

(c) Kinsale 1601: the Irish attempt to relieve the Spanish

Lord Mountjoy to the Council of Dublin, 26 December 1601
We doubt not but that you have long since heard that first [Hugh Roe] O'Donnell, after him Tyrone, and lastly [Richard] Tyrrell, with all the forces they could make, are drawn hither to relieve the
5   Spaniards at Kinsale, and to force us to raise our siege. They have lain before us a good while encamped in a fastness between the camps and Cork, and had gotten a good part of the Spaniards that landed lately at Castlehaven to join with them. Upon Christmas Even, being the 24 of December, in the morning before day, they
10   were by our scouts discovered to be marching towards the town in good order of battle, with the whole force of horse and foot. . . . But so it hath pleased Almighty God, to whom we wholly ascribe it, that not above three or four hundred of our horse, and two thousand of our foot, being drawn out to
15   encounter them, (for no more we could well spare, leaving our camps well guarded), made them retreat, whom we followed about two miles from our camp, and in the end charged them very resolutely upon a ford where they made a stand with their whole force, and gave them presently an overthrow, making their
20   horse and foot to run away, being not less than 5000, and the killing, as we judged of about 1200 of them. . . .
         Trevelyan Papers, op cit, pp 104–6

(d) Kinsale 1601: the Irish and Spanish are routed

. . . Tyrone, with O'Donnell and the rest of the Irish Lords, ran apace and so saved themselves. Those of the battle were almost all slain, and there were (of Irish rebels only) found dead in the place
25   about 1200 bodies, and about 800 more were hurt, whereof many died that night; and the chase continuing almost two miles, left off, our men being tired with killing. The enemy left 2000 arms brought to reckoning, beside great numbers embezzled away, all their powder and drums, and nine ensigns, whereof six were
30   Spanish. Those of the Irish that were taken prisoners, being brought to the camp, though they offered ransom were all hanged. On our side one only was slain, the cornet of Sir Richard Greame. . . .

And thus were they utterly overthrown, who but the night before
35   were so brave and confident of their good success, as they
reckoned us already theirs, and as we since have understood they
were in contention whose prisoner the Lord Deputy should be,
whose the Lord President, and so of the rest. . . .

After this good victory the Lord Deputy [Mountjoy] the same
40   day hastened to his camp, lest anything in his absence might be
attempted there.

The next day his Lordship commanded Captain Bedlogh, the
trenchmaster general of the camp, who as well in the fight as in
the works had deserved special commendation, to see the formerly
45   begun fort and plot formed to be undertaken again, and nearer
approaches to be cast out towards the town. But after five or six
days' labour, Don John (Don Juan del Aguila), captain of the town,
with forces within, offered a parley. . . . His request being
consented unto by his Lordship Sir William Godolphin was
50   employed in the negotiation . . . . [terms were concluded on
2 January 1602]

> Adams's *Chronicle of Bristol* (1623, Arrowsmith, 1910),
> pp 166–7

(e) Kinsale 1601: the Irish account

[Original in Erse.]

When the particular night upon which it was agreed they should
make this attack arrived, the Irish cheerfully and manfully put on
their dresses of battle and conflict, and were prepared for marching.
55   Their chiefs were at variance, each of them contending that he
himself should go foremost in the night's attack; so that the
manner in which they set out from the borders of their camp was
in three strong battalions, three extensive and numerous hosts,
shoulder to shoulder, and elbow to elbow. . . .

60   After they had marched outside their camp in this manner, the
forces mistook their road and lost their way, in consequence of the
great darkness of the night, so that their guides were not able to
make their way to the appointed place, opposite the camp of the
Lord Justice [Mountjoy] until clear daylight next morning. Some
65   assert that a certain Irishman had sent word and information to the
Lord Justice, that the Irish and Spaniards were to attack him that
night, and that, therefore, the Lord Justice and the Queen's army
stationed themselves in the gaps of danger, and certain other
passes, to defend the camp against their enemies. When the
70   darkness of the night had disappeared and the light of the day was
clear to all in general, it happened that O'Neill's [Tyrone's]
people, without being aware of it, had advanced near the Lord
Justice's people; but as they were not prepared, they turned aside
from them to be drawn up in battle array and order and to wait

75 for O'Donnell and the other party, who had lost their way, as we have before stated.

As soon as the Lord Justice perceived this thing, he sent forth vehement and vigorous troops to engage them so that they fell upon O'Neill's people, and proceeded to kill, slaughter, subdue and
80 thin them, until five or six ensigns were taken from them and many of their men were slain.

O'Donnell advanced to the side of O'Neill's people, after they were discomfited, and proceeded to call out to those who were flying, to stand their ground. . . . But however, all he did was of
85 no avail to him, for, as the first battalion was defeated, so were the others also in succession. But, although they were routed, the number of slain was not very great, on account of the fewness of the pursuers, in comparison with those [flying] before them.

Manifest was the displeasure of God . . . for previous to this
90 day, a small number of them had more frequently routed many hundreds of the English, than they had fled from them, in the field of battle. . . . Immense and countless was the loss in that place, although the number of slain was trifling; for the prowess and valour, prosperity and affluence, nobleness and chivalry, dignity
95 and renown, hospitality and generosity, bravery and protection, devotion and pure religion of the Island were lost in this engagement.

> *Annals of the Kingdom of Ireland by the four Masters*, ed. J. O'Donovan (1854), (reprinted A. M. S. Press Inc., 1966), vol VI, pp 2283–9

Questions

a In what ways does the Irish account differ from the English narratives, particularly in explaining the Irish defeat and estimating casualties?
b In your own words explain what the Irish chroniclers claim was at stake in this campaign.
★ c To what extent was the Irish question 'settled' by the end of Elizabeth's reign?

VIII 'Dangers great: many: imminent' – Diplomacy and War

Introduction

The first question about Elizabethan foreign policy is how far it was really a policy at all, and how far a reaction to events which Elizabeth could not have influenced in advance. The answer lies in a consideration of the constraints on the power of the English nation state: finance: manpower: ships and munitions: diplomats (the resident ambassador was still the exception – merchants and travelling nobles often doubled as spies and diplomats). Did these constraints make Elizabeth inclined to try to be one step ahead, or to temporise?

The first priority in early years was to work against French power in Scotland and the Low Countries. Philip II and Spain were not the 'natural' enemy at this time; Philip feared France, and Mary Stuart's claim to the English throne, more than he hated Elizabeth's heresy, while Elizabeth for her part needed Spain's neutrality at least.

How is it, then, that Spain becomes, later, the arch-enemy to such an emphatic degree that the stereotype of the 'cruel Dons' has been engraved in English Tudor History ever since? Two clues are, firstly, that enmity with Spain, when it came, meant enmity on a world-wide front, widening English horizons to the New World, and to areas where we sought to 'turn the flank' of Spain, such as Muscovy, Germany and the Levant. Secondly, whilst the religious divide in Europe was not always the main cleft between powers (consider the position of France), it became between Philip's Spain and Elizabeth's England a fundamental ideological schism which exacerbated all their dealings.

Yet, what was the real measure of England's ability to hurt Spain? Did she really have it in her to bring Spain to her knees, as the sea-dogs believed, or was England's role that of an incidental agent of decay in an overstretched Empire?

So serious were the crises of actual survival that for England to remain a sovereign nation state was itself the mark of a successful policy, and all else was a bonus. Furthermore, Elizabeth's failure to produce or nominate a successor tied England's survival uniquely to her own.

1 Dangers

(a) A memorandum by Lord Burghley, c. 1585

Dangers: 1: Great: 2: Many: 3: Imminent.

Great in respect of (a) the persons: the Q[ueen's] Majesty herself as patient. The Pope. The Kings of France and Spain. The Q[ueen] of Scots as the instrument whereby the perils do grow, (b) the
5   matters.

   Matters: (a) recovery of the tyrannous estate to the Church of Rome, which of late years has been in many parts weakened, and now so earnestly regarded by the two principal monarchies of Christendom, that is of France and Spain, as they have left all
10   other affairs, and buried all other quarrels and have made an open profession under the title of executing the Council of Trent [1563], to recover by sword the authority of the Pope: which matter was never in such earnest and plain sort attempted in this age before now.

15   (b) eviction of the Crown of England from the Q[ueen's] Majesty, to set it upon the head of the Q[ueen] of Scots, as a matter specially also tending to the purpose of the said two Monarch's attempts and enterprise.

   The recovery of the tyrannous estate of Rome cannot be
20   sufficiently accomplished, and to the contentment of the two monarchies, but by means of: (a) wars in France to make a full conquest of all Protestants there, and the like in Flanders and the Low Countries; (b) changing of the state of England to Popery, which cannot be accomplished whilst the Q[ueen's] Majesty lives
25   nor so assuredly and plausibly compassed, as by placing the Q[ueen] of Scots in the seat of this Crown. . . .

   The strength of the Q[ueen] of Scots and her friends stands at their present by (a) the universal opinion of all the States and sorts of people adhering to the Church of Rome in the justice of her
30   title: (b) the countenance, favour and maintenance of the greatest monarchies who after their own particular conquests, or rather jointly with them, will attempt to recover the Q[ueen] of Scots to her title; (c) the plausible opinion of a multitude [majority] both in Scotland and England that have an earnest disposition, and as it
35   were a natural 'instinction' to join both England and Scotland together, which cannot be but by means of the Q[ueen] of Scots.

   The weakness of the Q[ueen's] Majesty comes by (a) lack of marriage, children [or] alliance with foreign princes; (b) reason of long peace, and consequently ignorance of martial knowledge;
40   lack of a number of captains and leaders of soldiers; over-much boldness grown in a multitude of subjects upon opinion of the Q[ueen's] Majesty's remissness and favourable government, seeing no strait [i.e. strict] execution of her laws made for her surety;

45 (c) imperfections in lack of treasure; excess of all ordinary charges: poverty of the nobility and specially of all persons that are devoted to her service, the wealth being in the contrary sorts.

The *multitude* of the perils may be gathered of the premises and to number them particularly were too much offensive and uncomfortable.

50 *Imminency* of the former perils approaching may appear by (a) consideration of the causes of the prolongation of the perils until this time; (b) examination of the present perils and their nature.

The prolongation hitherto hath grown by the (a) accidents in France since the beginning of the Q[ueen's] Majesty's reign: the
55 death of King Henry of France: the dissension for government in his son King Francis's time, betwixt the Q[ueen] Mother and the King of Navarre: the death of K[ing] Francis whereby the Q[ueen] of Scots' titles were severed from the Crown of France: the inward troubles in France for matters of religion which have continued
60 now these [blank] years: (b) accidents in Scotland these eight or nine years; the discord betwixt the nation of Scotland and the French army: the 'unlucky' marriage of the Q[ueen] of Scots with the L[ord] Darnley: the division of the nobility for that marriage: the death and murder of the Said L[ord] Darnley, wherewith the
65 Q[ueen] being charged, her son was crowned, whereupon the civil dissension continues, not without peril to the State of England if Hamilton recover his purpose.

Calender of the MSS of the Marquis of Salisbury, vol XIII, Addenda, pp 288–90

(b) Eve's seditious libel

('Eve' or 'Ewe' was apparently an Englishman who espoused the Catholic and Irish causes like Sir Thomas Stukeley. Both were
70 Devon men.) Published in Waterford (Ireland), and by the Mayor sent to the Lord Justice, 25 July 1580 . . . .

From Rome, 23 February, 1580

On Thursday last the Ambassadors of the King Catholic [of Spain] and the Duke of Florence were admitted to an audience
75 together [with Pope Gregory XIII], and at the same time the league was concluded against the Queen of England between his Holiness and the said King and the Duke of Florence in manner and form following, viz:

'That his Holiness will furnish 10,000 footmen and 1000
80 horsemen; the King Catholic, 15,000 footmen and 1500 horsemen; the Duke of Florence 8000 footmen and 100 horsemen; to which armies shall be joined the Germans which are already passed into Spain: they to be paid rateably [in proportion] by the said princes.

That if it shall please our Lord God to give a happy voyage and
85 success to the army, that, before any other thing else, the people

may be warned in his Holiness' name to return to the Catholic Roman church, and to live in obedience thereof, in such manner and form as their predecessors have done before this time.

90 That his Holiness, as Sovereign Lord of the island, will grant to the noblemen Catholic of the country to make election of [a] Catholic Lord of the island, who with his authority of the See Apostolic shall be declared King; provided always that he shall be always obedient and faithful to the See Apostolic, as the Catholic kings have done until the time of their last Henry.

95 That the Queen Elizabeth shall be declared a wrongful detainer and unable to hold the kingdom, for being born of unlawful marriage, and also that she is an heretic.

That the goods of the churches shall be returned out of the hands of those which occupy the same; and that good and wise 100 men of the country be created bishops and abbots and such like, who with the example of their life and with preaching may reduce the people to the religion.

That the King of Spain shall not pretend anything otherwise than to make league and alliance, if he will, with the King so to be 105 chosen. . . .

That the Q[ueen] of S[cots] shall be set at liberty, and helped again to her own kingdom, if she had need.

That his Holiness will treat with the French King, to the end that neither he, nor Monsieur [the Duke of Anjou] his brother 110 shall help the Queen nor Flemings against Spain.

That the bull of excommunication which Pius V, of happy memory, did give out against the same Queen [1570], shall be published in every church and Christian Court.

That the Catholic Englishmen be received into the army, and 115 convenient pay given them according to the qualities of the persons. . . .

Calendar of the Carew MSS, 1575–1588, pp 288–9

Questions

★ a How true was it, circa 1585, to say that France and Spain had 'left all other affairs' to restore Papal authority in England (lines 9–10)?

★ b Which monarch would have had a greater desire to see Mary Stuart on the English throne – the King of France or the King of Spain?

c Comment on the phrase, 'a multitude (majority) . . . have . . . a natural "instinction" to join both England and Scotland together' (lines 33–36).

d Suggest reasons why Burghley may have been overpessimistic in assessing England's weaknesses in extract *a*, lines 37–46.

e   Burghley interprets the troubles in France since 1558 as a source of England's troubles. Do you interpret them in the same light?

★ f   What was 'unlucky' about Mary Stuart's marriage with Darnley (line 62)?

★ g   What was (James) Hamilton (of Arran)'s 'purpose' (line 67)?

h   Why did some Catholic hopes for the deposition of Elizabeth centre on Ireland?

★ i   Outline the main points of Pius V's bull of 1570 (extract b, line 111).

★ j   Why should the libel report that the King of Spain disclaimed the throne of Ireland? Who would have wished to be reassured of this?

★ k   In what ways had the King of France, Anjou and Elizabeth been helping the Flemings against Spain (extract b, lines 109–110)?

l   From the evidence in extracts a and b, suggest how realistic Elizabeth's ministers' fears of the Catholic world were.

2   France

This year [1559] both the Kings [of Spain and France] sent their deputies to Cateau Cambrésis, about six leagues from Cambrai, to which place the Queen of England sent her commissioners, and so did the Duke of Savoy. The Duchess of Lorraine came thither in
5   person, accompanied with the young Duke, her son, by whose honest endeavours to compound a peace between these parties by persuasion, by entreaties, by all other moderate means, has gained to her a perpetual honour in the annals and histories of all these nations. At the last all differences were accorded except the
10   restitution of Calais to the English, which was both stiffly demanded by King Philip and denied by the French. . . . But when they saw that without performance of this condition, nothing could be done, they studied only how they might for the present defer it, knowing right well that time works many
15   advantages which neither are contrived, nor can be conceived at the first. To this purpose they employed Guido Cavalcanti, a gentleman of Florence, by whose means a special treaty was entertained between the Queen of England and the French king. And so effectually did Cavalcanti deal, that in short time, it was
20   concluded that Calais should remain in possession of the French king for the term of eight years; that, this term being expired, he should render the same to the Queen of England, or else to forfeit to her the sum of 500,000 crowns; that for surety of the performance hereof, he should deliver four such hostages to the
25   Queen as she should think fit. . . .

It is very like[ly] that the Queen by consideration of her new and unsettled estate, the less assured by reason of the great mutation which she had made, and partly for that she had some cause of jealousy [i.e. fear] lest the French king and the King of
30 Spain (especially for the cause of religion) might be driven to make a peace prejudicial to her.

> Sir John Hayward, *Annals of the first four years of the reign of Queen Elizabeth*, ed. J. Bruce (Camden Society, 1840), pp 34–5

Questions

* *a* Outline the events leading to the Treaty of Cateau Cambrésis.
 b Why did Philip II take England's part so 'stiffly' (line 10)?
 c Name two people commended for their diplomacy in this extract.
* *d* When and why did Elizabeth subsequently forfeit her claim to Calais?
 e What 'great mutation' (lines 27–28) had Elizabeth made?
* *f* How do you account for the fact that France ceased to be England's principal continental enemy in subsequent decades?

3 Rebellion against Spain

(a) An appeal to the Queen, c. 1572

The Governor and others of Flushing [Vlissingen, Holland], to the Queen:

As it is clearly seen that the Duke of Alva pursues the ruin and desolation of the Low Countries, they have refused entry to the
5 Spaniards, taking arms for the preservation of the town, under the authority of the King of Spain their natural prince. With the town are joined the towns of Campveere and Arnemuiden, and all the Isle of Walcheren, except Middelburg. They have done violence to none, holding only for enemies the said Duke and his Spaniards,
10 as disturbers of the public peace. In testimony whereof they have let pass freely a Spanish fleet going to the Low Countries, without touching either money or goods, excepting only powder and artillery of which they had great need. Since then, being pressed by the violence of their enemies it is impossible for them to
15 maintain their sea forces, feed their soldiers and supply munitions of war and fortifications, without ruining the adjacent countries subject to the King of Spain, which they would do with great regret. They have therefore sent Jacques de Surigher their burgher, to pray the Queen to lend them money to preserve their town and
20 country.

> *Calendar of the MSS of the Marquis of Salisbury, op cit, p 115*

(b) An appeal to the queen, 1587

M.B. to the Queen (Original in Italian.)
20 August 1587

Madame, I will once more, and for the last time, obey the passion which generates in me the affection I bear for your
25 Majesty and your affairs, and tell you that when you first took the protection of the Low Countries I sought to show you that the places there appeared to be strong but were not really so, and that where they are strongest by nature they should by art be made safe from assault and then provided with every necessary for
30 holding them against a long siege by armies. . . .

. . . If I were an Englishman I could say that no one is a prophet in his own country; but from personal experience I will say that in England a foreigner is neither believed nor valued, and it annoys me more for your service than for myself, especially as my
35 opinion has been confirmed by the capture of Sluys with less than 10,000 men, only because it was not suitably provided. If any place in those countries was capable of being rendered impregnable it was Sluys – in spite of many valiant defenders it was lost because proper measures had not been taken and it was ill provided
40 with powder. . . .

Your Majesty's resolution to maintain an armada at sea is very praiseworthy and may do much good if only for your reputation and the expense to which it will put the King of Spain in the escorting of his fleets. Moreover it will be a sentinel to your
45 kingdom and may find opportunity to capture the whole or part of one of the fleets, or to defeat the enemy's armada: and it cannot do so little as not to win its expenses. . . .

Paris, 20 August 1587

Calendar of the MSS of the Marquis of Salisbury, op cit, pp 345–6

Questions

★　a　What events in the Low Countries preceded the supposed date of extract *a*?
　　b　How do the Dutch rebels' references to Spain's Sovereignty in the Netherlands change from extract *a* to extract *b*?
★　c　What reasons did Elizabeth have for being reluctant to help the Dutch rebels? (There are clues to some of her reasons in the extracts.)
★　d　Who was the captor of Sluys in 1587? Why did Elizabeth have cause to fear his presence in the Netherlands, as she had done that of the Duke of Alva?
★　e　Comment on the author of extract *b*'s assessment of Elizabeth's naval policy in 1587.

(c) The Portuguese venture

[Don Antonio] to Queen Elizabeth

I arrived here the first of this month and God knows how much more gladly I would have reached Dover. I found Count Stabbe and Filippo Estroci, and Santa Solena most resolute to follow my
5   fortune, and on behalf of many French gentlemen they made me the same offer. From the King of France and his mother they offered me all that I could have wished. I have put off any decision as to my conduct until I can speak with their Majesties, and in the meantime I would beg your Majesty to advise me as to what I
10   ought to do, for you alone are my guide and my mistress.

You know what harm the enmity of the Spaniards can do to your realm, how worthy of your greatness it is to help one who loves and worships you and is ready to die for you.

Dieppe, 3rd October [1588?]
15   Sealed with the Arms of Portugal.

Calendar of the MSS of the Marquis of Salisbury, op cit, p 383

Questions

★   a   Who was Don Antonio?
★   b   What were the purposes of the English expeditions to Portugal in 1589? Was this an extension of English policy or a new departure? What was the outcome?
    c   Comment on the words, 'You know what harm the enmity of the Spaniards can do to your realm . . .' (lines 11–12).

4   Defence against Spain

(a) Trained bands

A letter from the Lords of the Council touching horsemen and footmen, dated 2 August 1586

After our right hearty commendations to your Lo[rdship] [the Earl of Pembroke, President of the Council of Wales, Lord
5   Lieutenant of Somerset and Wiltshire], her Majesty's having of late entered into consideration how necessary it were for sundry good respects that such orders as the last year were taken as well for the training of horsemen and footmen as in diverse other things touching to the defence of the Realm should be this year
10   renewed, has willed us to signify to you that forasmuch the harvest time draws on it has been thought meet that the time of the view and training of the foot Bands should be referred to your Lo[rdshi]p's consideration who can best judge how the same may be performed by the apt choice of time with the least burden
15   and grief to the subjects. And for that the training of the shot is

the chief matter wherein most travail [effort] would be taken, and some more time would be spent than in the rest of the Band: we do not see but that if according to the orders set down the last year, the shot in every Band be trained by the Corporal in the
20   several Bands after evening prayers in the holy days, the same may be done with the good intentment of all well affected subjects, and in case choice be made of men of ability to serve in the said Bands according to the instructions given in the same behalf; then may the same be performed without any taxation or
25   burden to the country. And whereas we are informed that diverse [men] well affected to this public service, to the end they may not be placed in the said Bands, are become retainers to certain noblemen, gentlemen and haply [perhaps] to some of us; we think meet that none of the said retainers to whomsoever they belong
30   should be exempt from this public service. . . .

Somerset Record Office, DD/PH 220

(b) Beacons

Order agreed upon by the Lord Lieutenant of the County of Devon and his deputy the 10th of July 1588 to be published generally within the limits of their Lieutenancy.

Item: for the better and more perfect order in watching of the
35   beacons it is thought necessary that none be appointed to watch-and-ward but such as are discreet and sufficient persons; and those that are appointed to watch by night to repair to the constable or tithingman as the same is ready to receive the watchword and immediately to go and continue at the place appointed for the said
40   watch until the sun rises the next day, and then to return again to the constable or tithingman, and deliver up their watchword, who presently shall appoint some other to ward the place all the day following; and if any person so appointed to watch or ward shall be found faulty or negligent in the said service they shall by the
45   L[ord] Lieutenant or his deputies or the Justices of Peace next adjoining be committed to prison and receive such other punishment as to their discretion shall be thought meet.

By Sir Robert Denys: Instructions for the head constables of the Hundred of Colyton: . . . A small beacon allow by the waterside
50   to be made, the said beacon to be watched day and night by such men of good discretion, three by night and one by day.

Item: if any head Constable, petty Constable or tithingman shall be found negligent in doing their duties for the advancement of her Majesty's service, that the [each] and every one of them so
55   offending shall be imprisoned by the space of ten days or more as shall be thought convenient to the L[ord] Lieutenant or his deputies according to the quality of his or their offence.

Somerset Record Office, DD/WO 55/7

Questions

  a Using the information given in extract *a* as evidence, what difficulties existed in keeping the trained bands in a state of readiness and proficiency?

  b What is the relationship between periods of training or retraining and harvest-time?

  c How did some men seek to evade service in the trained bands?

★ *d* Which of the defence measures provided for in the extracts were actually used in the events of 1588?

5 The Spanish Armada

The next year [1588] the King of Spain's great Armada came upon our coast, thinking to devour us all. Upon the news sent to court from Plymouth of their certain arrival, my Lord [the Earl of] Cumberland and myself took post horse and rode straight to
5 Portsmouth, where we found a frigate that carried us to sea; and having sought the fleets a whole day, the night after we fell amongst them, where it was our fortune to light first upon the Spanish fleet: and finding ourselves in the wrong, we tacked about, and in short time got to our own fleet, which was not far
10 from the other . . . . It was on Thursday [25 July] that we came to the fleet. All that day we followed close the Spanish Armada, and nothing was attempted on either side; the same course we held all Friday and Saturday, by which time the Spanish fleet cast anchor just before Calais. We likewise did the same, a very small distance
15 behind them, and so continued till Monday morning about two of the clock: in which time our council of war had provided six [some witnesses say eight] old hulks and stuffed them full of all combustible matter fit for burning, and on Monday at two in the morning they were let loose, with each of them a man in her to
20 direct them. The tide serving, they brought them very near the Spanish fleet, so that they could not miss to come amongst the midst of them: then they set fire on them, and came off themselves, having each of them a little boat to bring him off. The ships set on fire came so directly to the Spanish fleet as they had no way to
25 avoid them, but to cut all their hawsers and so escape; . . . They being in this disorder, we made ready to follow them, where began a cruel fight, and we had such advantage, both of wind and tide, as we had a glorious day of them, continuing fight from four o'clock in the morning till almost five or six at night, where they
30 lost a dozen or fourteen of their best ships, some sunk and the rest run ashore in diverse parts to keep themselves from sinking. After God had given us this great victory, they made all the haste they could away, and we followed them Tuesday and Wednesday, by which time they were gotten as far as Flamborough Head. It

35   was resolved on Wednesday at night that by four o'clock on
Thursday we should have a near fight with them for a farewell;
but by two in the morning there was a flag of council hung out in
our Vice Admiral, when it was found that in the whole fleet there
was not munition sufficient to make half a fight; and therefore it
40   was there concluded that we should let them pass, and our fleet to
return to the Downs. . . .

> *The Memoirs of Robert Carey*, ed. F. H. Mares (1972),
> pp 9–10

Questions

   a   What evidence does Carey's account give us of the dispositions
       of the English and Spanish fleets in the English Channel?

★ *b*   To what does Carey attribute the successes of the English?
       What factors not mentioned by Carey would you add to the
       reckoning?

   c   What evidence is there in the extract that the English were
       barely prepared for a full-scale naval encounter with the
       Spanish?

6   Drake and Hawkins Beyond the Line

(a) Drake in the Pacific

From Gaspar de Vargas, Chief 'Alcalde' of the Port of Guatulco
[Mexican Pacific coast], 13 April 1579. [Original in Spanish.]

   This morning of Holy Monday . . . I was informed by some
sailors of a ship belonging to Juan Madrid . . . that they had just
5   seen two sails very near to the entrance of port . . . . Two hours
later, at about ten o'clock, both ships began to enter the port
abreast, and it became apparent that the larger one was, as
everyone says, of more than 300 tons. The other one also appeared
to be larger than had first been said. They entered the port with
10   great determination and the larger ship cast anchor. The bark,
which turned out to be a launch, and the ship's boat, filled with
men, began to come very suddenly in a resolute manner, towards
the shore. Then only was it understood that it was the English
Corsair that he turned out to be. [It was Drake.]
15   I went to meet them on the shore with the few Spaniards and
some Indians who were decorating the church for Holy Thursday
and Easter. With the weapons that we found, we prepared to
oppose their landing insofar that the boat, which carried more
than forty archers and gunners, was delayed until the launch
20   began to discharge its artillery, which was supported by the
arquebuses in the boat. It then became necessary for us to abandon
the town and retire up the hill, from the heights of which we

discharged our arquebuses. We saw them land, and with their captain, begin to plunder the property of the merchants and of those of us who live there. What is most and above all else to be deplored is the shamelessness with which they, with their knives, hacked into pieces the sacred images and crucifixes, after which, laden with plunder, they returned to their ship . . . .

As far as we could see they carried off three persons, who were the curate, his relative the mayor of Suchitepec, named Miranda, who had come to spend Holy Week in the port, and a certain Francisco Gomez, factor . . . .

I . . . have just arrived here at ten o'clock at night, so as to send Your Excellency this dispatch by a suitable person who can reach Oaxaca in two and a half or three days and thence send another on . . . .

From this same place I sent another Spaniard to San Juan Acapulco, a hundred leagues from here, so that even if he has to kill horses in doing so, he can reach that port before the ship, so that the necessary precautions can be taken.

Your Excellency might be served . . . if, in all haste, 400 men could be shipped in the large vessel belonging to Juan Diaz, and in his Majesty's ship. They could await this Corsair or go out to meet and grapple with him. Doubtless they would obtain a certain victory over him . . . .

> *New Light on Drake*, trans. Zelia Nuttall (Hakluyt Society, second series, vol 34, 1914), pp 213–15

(b) Drake's and Hawkins' last voyage

'[Sept. 24, 1595]: The 24th day in the afternoon we descried land which was Fuerteventura and Lanzarote: we lay becalmed at hull until four of the clock next morning and then we set sail, and the 25th day we were to the northwards of the Canaries, and so we stood it back to the southward and came into the road, where we anchored at 8 or 9 fathom water; and we manned our boats to land our men between a block house and the town. But the Spaniards had trenched themselves close by one shore so strongly that we could not land our men without the loss of a great many of them. 13 or 14 of our ships went in close by the shore and played upon them, then the generals, seeing no good to be done there, commanded us all aboard our ships again and set sail. We had 12 or 13 men slain and hurt . . . .

[Sept. 29]: The night before Sir Francis Drake and five ships more had lost Sir John Hawkins and the rest of the fleet, and sailed along by Dominica to an island called Marie Galante, where anchored and went ashore: the savages' people ran away: Sir Francis Drake rode after and spoke with some of them, but could find nothing, nor good water. Then we sailed five leagues further

65 to an island called Guadeloupe, where we cast anchor on the north
side near the shore at 20 or 30 fathoms, where we had good
watering, and built part of our pinnaces. The day after the rest of
the fleet came to us, but they had lost the 'Francis' of Greenwich,
which had met with five of the King of Spain's men of war that
70 took her and carried news of our coming to St. John [San Juan]
Puerto Rico . . . .
[Nov. 13] The 13th day within sight of Puerto Rico Sir John
Hawkins died; and that afternoon we anchored in a bay one league
eastward from the town where the Spaniards had planted great
75 ordnance, and played upon our ships, and killed Sir Nicholas
Clifford aboard our admiral, and hurt Capt. Stratford and Mr.
Browne who died shortly after, and struck the stool from under
Sir Francis Drake being all at supper together . . . .
[Nov. 14]: That night we manned our pinnaces and boats, and
80 went to burn these five ships which had taken the 'Francis': one of
them we burned and set another on fire, but the fort played so
sore upon us that they discharged 178 great shot at our boats.
They killed and hurt of us together 140 men . . . .
[Dec. 1]: The first of December all our land men were put into
85 pinnaces and sailed all along the shore by a little town called
Rancheria towards Rio de la Hach. But they had intelligence by a
carvel that was sent all along the [Spanish] Main of our coming,
so that they conveyed away all their goods and treasure up into
the country . . . .
90 [Dec. 27 at Nombre de Dios] . . . the Spaniards made a volley
of small shot at us, and discharged a minion [3 inch gun] at us
from the fort, and then ran all away: the minion broke in pieces,
so we took the town without loss. There were some sows of
silver and gold, plate and velvet found hidden in the woods, but
95 they had conveyed most part of their goods into the country up to
Panama, for they had likewise intelligence of our coming three
weeks before . . . .
[Jan. 27 1596]: On Tuesday Sir Francis Drake died: on the next
day he was enclosed in lead and cast into the deep . . . .'
100 So much and no more I found in two of their copies: they came
home very sick and weak for the most part.
    Adams's Chronicle of Bristol (1623, Arrowsmith, 1910),
    pp 144–9

Questions

a In what ways is it shown that the authorities in Guatulco were
    taken unawares by Drake's arrival (extract *a*)?

b What action of the English in extract *a* was deplored most by
    the Spanish?

★ c Trace the subsequent fortunes of Drake on the American Pacific coast. Were Gaspar de Varga's actions and recommendations appropriate or adequate?

d Using the information given in extract *b* as evidence, say in how many ways Spanish measures against English raids were more effective in the 1590's than they had been in the 1580's? Does extract *b* bear out Sir Walter Raleigh's opinion that 'her Majesty did all by halves and by petty invasion taught the Spaniard how to defend himself'?

e What misfortunes apart from Spanish resistance did the 1595–96 venture face?

Vice General de Viñas, action and accommodation
principals of adequate
... the ... that is ...
... and ... that the ... but ...
you ... be than St. Paul. It be banished for per-
... all believers ... part manner made the
... how to deal of ...
... operation apart from the ... reason and rust
... and face